THE HOLY HOUR
PRAYER BOOK

"COULD YOU NOT WATCH
ONE HOUR WITH ME"

MEDITATIONS AND REFLECTIONS

FULTON J. SHEEN

Bishop Sheen Today
280 John Street
Midland, Ontario, Canada
L4R 2J5

www.bishopsheentoday.com

Cover design by Janika Barman
www.twitter.com/barman_janika

On the cover: Picture of the Sacred Host in the monstrance,
placed on the main altar at the Cathedral of St. Mary of the
Immaculate Conception located in Peoria, Illinois during
Eucharistic Adoration. (Courtesy of Phillip Lee)
www.cdop.org

Library of Congress Cataloging-in-Publication Data

Names: Sheen, Fulton J. (Fulton John), 1895-1979, author.
| Smith, Allan J., editor.

Sheen, Fulton J. (Fulton John), 1895-1979. The Holy Hour:
Reading and Prayers for a Daily Hour of Meditation.
Prepared for the National Council of Catholic Men.
Huntington,IN: Our Sunday Visitor, (1946)

The Armor of God: Reflections and Prayers for Wartime.
Registered in the name of P. J.Kenedy and Sons under
Library Congress catalog card number: A 174944, following
publication July 15, 1943

Smith, Al (Allan J.) editor – Lord Teach us to Pray: A Fulton
Sheen Anthology. Manchester, New Hampshire: Sophia
Institute Press, 2019, ISBN 9781644130834.

Title: The Holy Hour Prayer Book. "Could you not watch one
hour with me." Meditations and Reflections by Fulton J.
Sheen.

Fulton J. Sheen; compiled by Allan J. Smith.

Description: Midland, Ontario: Bishop Sheen Today, 2021

Identifiers: ISBN: 978-1-990427-18-3 (paperback)
ISBN: 978-1-990427-19-0 (eBook)
ISBN: 978-1-990427-71-8 (hardcover)

Includes bibliographical references.

Subjects: Jesus Christ — The Holy Hour — Prayer and
Meditation

TABLE OF CONTENTS

THE HOLY HOUR: MEDITATIONS AND REFLECTIONS

"Could You Not Watch One Hour With Me."

PRAYERS OF MEDITATION AND PETITION

WHY MAKE A HOLY HOUR?

The purpose of these meditations is to aid souls in securing an inner peace by meditating one continuous hour a day on God and our immortal destiny. Whether or not one uses these meditations does not matter in the least. Some Jews, some Protestants, and some Catholics may find it very unsatisfactory. If, however, they reject these because they wish to make the Holy Hour in their own way, they will have achieved its purpose. What is vital, is not that these meditations be used, but that there be meditation.

But why spend an hour a day in meditation? Because we are living on the surface of our souls, knowing little either of God or our inner self. Our knowledge is mostly about things, not about destiny. Most of our difficulties and disappointments in life are due to mistakes in our life plans. Having forgotten the purpose of living, we have doubted even the value of living. A broken bone gives pain because it is not where it ought to be; our souls are in agony because we are not tending to the fullness of Life, Truth, and Love, which is God.

But why make a Holy Hour? Here are ten reasons.

(1) Because it is time spent in the Presence of Our Lord Himself. If faith is alive, no further reason is needed.

(2) Because in our busy life it takes considerable time to shake off the "noonday devils," the worldly cares, which cling to our souls, like dust. An hour with Our Lord follows the experience of the disciples on the road to Emmaus (Luke 24:13-35). We begin by walking with Our Lord, but our eyes are "held fast" so that we do not "recognize him"'. Next, He converses with our soul, as we read the Scriptures. The third stage is one of sweet intimacy, as when 'he sat down at table with them.' The fourth stage is the full dawning of the mystery of the Eucharist. Our eyes are "opened," and we recognize Him. Finally, we reach the point where we do not want to leave. The hour seemed so short. As we arise, we ask:

Were not our hearts burning within us
when he spoke to us on the road, and when he
made the Scriptures plain to us? (Luke 24:32)

(3) Because Our Lord asked for it.

Had you no strength, then, to watch with
me even for an hour? (Matt. 26:40)

The word was addressed to Peter, but he is
referred to as Simon. It is our Simon-nature,
which needs the hour. If the hour seems hard, it
is because ... the spirit is willing enough, but the
flesh is weak. (Mark 14:39)

(4) Because the Holy Hour keeps a balance
between the spiritual and the practical. Western
philosophies tend to an activism in which God
does nothing, and man everything; the Eastern
philosophies tend to a quietism in which God
does everything, and man nothing. The golden
mean is in the words of St. Thomas: "action
following rest," Martha walking with Mary. The
Holy Hour unites the contemplative to the active
life of the person.

Thanks to the hour with Our Lord, our
meditations and resolutions pass from the

conscious to the subconscious and then become motives of action. A new spirit begins to pervade our work. The change is effected by Our Lord, Who fills our heart and works through our hands. A person can give only what he possesses. To give Christ to others, one must possess Him.

(5) Because the Holy Hour will make us practice what we preach.

Here is an image, he said, of the kingdom of heaven; there was once a king, who held a marriage feast for his son, and sent out his servants with a summons to all those whom he had invited to the wedding; but they would not come. (Matt. 22:2, 3)

It was written of Our Lord that He 'set out to do and to teach' (Acts 1:1). The person who practices the Holy Hour will find that when he teaches, the people will say of him as of the Lord:

All ... were astonished at the gracious words which came from his mouth. (Luke 4:22)

(6) Because the Holy Hour helps us make reparation both for the sins of the world and for

4

our own. When the Sacred Heart appeared to St. Margaret Mary, it was His Heart, and not His Head, that was crowned with thorns. It was Love that was hurt. Black Masses, sacrilegious communions, scandals, militant atheism – who will make up for them? Who will be an Abraham for Sodom, a Mary for those who have no wine? The sins of the world are our sins as if we had committed them. If they caused Our Lord a bloody sweat, to the point that He upbraided His disciples for failing to stay with Him an hour, shall we with Cain ask:

Is it for me to watch over my brother? (Gen. 4:9)

(7) Because it reduces our liability to temptation and weakness. Presenting ourselves before Our Lord in the Blessed Sacrament is like putting a tubercular patient in good air and sunlight. The virus of our sins cannot long exist in the face of the Light of the world.

Always I can keep the Lord within sight; always he is at my right hand, to make me stand firm. (Psalm 15:8)

5

Our sinful impulses are prevented from arising through the barrier erected each day by the Holy Hour. Our will becomes disposed to goodness with little conscious effort on our part. Satan, the roaring lion, was not permitted to put forth his hand to touch righteous Job until he received permission (Job 1:12). Certainly then will the Lord withhold serious fall from him who watches (1 Cor. 10:13). With full confidence in his Eucharistic Lord, the person will have a spiritual resiliency. He will bounce back quickly after a falling: Fall I, it is but to rise again, sit I in darkness, the Lord will be my light. The Lord's displeasure I must bear, I that have sinned against him, till at last, he admits my plea, and grants redress. (Micah 7:8, 9)

The Lord will be favorable even to the weakest of us, if He finds us at His feet in adoration, disposing ourselves to receive Divine favors. No sooner had Saul of Tarsus, the persecutor, humbled himself before his Maker, than God sent a special messenger to his relief, telling him that 'even now he is at his prayers' (Acts 9:11). Even the person who has fallen can expect reassurance if he watches and prays.

They shall increase, that hitherto had dwindled, be exalted, that once were brought low. (Jer. 30:19, 20)

(8) Because the Holy Hour is a personal prayer, the person, who limits himself strictly to his official obligation, is like the union man who downs tools the moment the whistle blows. Love begins when duty finishes. It is a giving of the cloak when the coat is taken. It is walking the extra mile.

Answer shall come ere cry for help is uttered; prayer find audience while it is yet on their lips. (Isa. 65:24)

Of course, we do not have to make a Holy Hour – and that is just the point. Love is never compelled, except in hell. There love has to submit to justice. To be forced to love would be a kind of hell. No man who loves a woman is obligated to give her an engagement ring, and no person who loves the Sacred Heart ever has to give an engagement Hour.

"Would you, too, go away?" (John 6:68) is *weak* love; "Art thou sleeping?" (Mark 14:37) is *irresponsible* love; "He had great possessions" (Matt. 19:22; Mark 10:22) is *selfish* love. But does the person who loves His Lord have time for other activities before he performs acts of love "above and beyond the call of duty"? Does the patient love the physician who charges for every call, or does he begin to love when the physician says: "I just dropped by to see how you were"?

(9) Meditation keeps us from seeking an external escape from our worries and miseries. When difficulties arise, when nerves are made taut by false accusations, there is always a danger that we may look outwards, as the Israelites did, for release.

From the Lord God, the Holy One of Israel, word was given you, Come back and keep still, and all shall be well with you; in quietness and in confidence lies your strength. But you would have none of it; To horse! you cried, We must flee! and flee you shall; We must ride swiftly, you said, but swifter still ride your pursuers. (Isa. 30:15, 16)

No outward escape, neither pleasure, drink, friends or keeping busy, is an answer. The soul cannot "fly upon a horse"; he must take "wings" to a place where his "life is hidden away ... with Christ in God" (Col. 3:3).

(10) Finally, because the Holy Hour is necessary for the Church. No one can read the Old Testament without becoming conscious of the presence of God in history. How often did God use other nations to punish Israel for her sins! He made Assyria the "rod that executes my vengeance" (Isa. 10:5). The history of the world since the Incarnation is the Way of the Cross. The rise of nations and their fall remain related to the Kingdom of God. We cannot understand the mystery of God's government, for it is the "sealed book" of the Apocalypse. John wept when he saw it (Rev. 5:4). He could not understand why this moment of prosperity and that hour of adversity.

The sole requirement is the venture of faith, and the reward is the depths of intimacy for those who cultivate His friendship. To abide with Christ is spiritual fellowship, as He insisted on the solemn and sacred night of the Last Supper, the moment He chose to give us the Eucharist:

You have only to live on in me, and I will live on in you. (John 15:4)

He wants us in His dwelling: That you, too, may be where I am. (John 14:3)

✠ J.M.J. ✠

HOW TO MAKE
THE HOLY HOUR

"Let nothing hinder thee from praying always, and be not afraid to be justified even to death for the rewards of God continue forever. Before prayer prepare thy soul; and be not as a man that tempt God" (Sir. 18; 22-23).

Prayer is the lifting of our soul to God unto the end of perfectly corresponding to His Holy Will. Our Divine Lord, describing His Mission, said: "For I have come down from heaven, not to do my own will, but the will of him who sent me ... the Father, that I should lose nothing of what he has given me, but that I should raise it up on the last day" (John 6:38, 39). "My food is to do the will of him who sent me, to accomplish his work" (John 4:34).

To correspond to the Divine Will, we must, first of all, know it, and secondly, have the grace and strength to correspond with it, once it is known. But to attain these two gifts of light for our minds and power for our wills, we must live on terms of intimate friendship with God. This is done through prayer. A prayerful life is, therefore, one lived in conformity with the Holy Will of God as a prayerless life is a life of self-will and selfishness.

There is an element of prayer common to Jews, Protestants, and Catholics, namely, belief in God. Above half of the prayers, for example, which a priest says in his Divine Office, are taken from the Old Testament. In relation to all three, that is Jews, Protestants, and Catholics; a Holy Hour will, therefore, be understood as one Hour a day spent in meditating on God and our eternal salvation. This Holy Hour can be made anywhere.

For Catholics, however, the Holy Hour has a very special significance. It means a continuous and unbroken Hour spent in the presence of Our Divine Lord in the Eucharist; for which reason a meditation on the Blessed Eucharist has been included as one of these meditations in this book.

In the case of priests and religious, it is suggested that they make this Holy Hour in addition to their usual recitation of the Divine Office and Holy Mass.

This Holy Hour will be spent in prayer and meditation. A distinction is here made between the two, with the emphasis on the latter. By prayer, we here understand the recitation of formal prayers, generally composed by a person different from him who prays.

The Psalms represent one of the highest forms of vocal prayer and are common to Jews, Protestants, and Catholics. Other vocal prayers include the Our Father, Hail Mary, Creed, Confiteor, Acts of Faith, Hope, and Charity, and thousands of other prayers found in religious books. There are three kinds of attention in vocal prayer: (1) to the words, lest we say them wrong; (2) to their sense and meaning; and (3) to God and the intention for which we pray. The last kind of attention is essential to vocal prayer.

But the principal purpose of these Holy Hour meditations is the cultivation of mental prayer or meditation. Very few souls ever meditate; they are either frightened by the word or else never taught its existence. In the human order, a person in love is always conscious of the one loved, lives in the presence of the other, resolves to do the will of the other, and regards as his greatest jealousy being outdone in the least advantage of self-giving. Apply this to a soul in love with God, and you have the rudiments of meditation.

Meditation is, therefore, a kind of communing of spirit with spirit, with God as its object. Without attempting to set down the formal aspects of meditation, but to make it as intelligible as possible to beginners, the technique of meditation is as follows:

(1) We speak to God: We begin by putting ourselves in the presence of God. For those who make the Holy Hour before the Blessed Sacrament, there must be a consciousness of our presence before the Body, Blood, Soul, and Divinity of Our Lord and Saviour Jesus Christ. Naturally, there are varying degrees of intimacy with persons. In a theatre, there are hundreds present, but little or no intimacy between them. The intimacy deepens to the degree that we establish conversation with one or more of them,

and according as this conversation springs from a common interest. So it is with God.

Prayer, then, is not a mere asking for things, but an aiming at a transformation; that is, a becoming "conformed to the image of his Son" (Rom. 8:29). We pray not to dispose God to give us something, but to dispose ourselves to receive something from Him: the fullness of Divine Life.

(2) God speaks to us: Activity is not only on human side but also on the Divine. A conversation is an exchange, not a monologue. As the soul willed to draw near God, God wills to draw near the soul. It would be wrong to monopolize the conversation with friends; it is more wrong to do so in our relations with God. We must not do all the talking; we must also be good listeners. "Speak Lord, for thy servant heareth" (1 Kings 3:9).

The soul now experiences the truth of the words "Draw near to God, and he will draw near to you" (James 4:8). All during the meditation, it will conceive devout affections of adoration, petition, sacrifice, and reparation to God, but particularly at the close of the meditation. These affections or colloquies are to be offered preferably in our own language, for every soul must make its own love to God, and God loves each soul in a particular manner.

"In the beginning, the soul attracted to Jesus by some impulse of grace, comes to Him, filled with natural thoughts and aspirations, and very ignorant of the supernatural. It understands neither God nor itself. It has a few intimate relations with the Divinity outside of itself and within itself, but it begins to converse with Jesus. If it persists in the frequentation of His company, the Lord gradually takes an ever-increasing share in the conversation and begins to enlighten the soul. In its contemplation of the mysteries of faith, He aids it to penetrate beneath the words and facts and symbols, hitherto known but superficially, and to grasp the inner sense of the supernatural truths contained in these facts or words or symbols. The Scriptures are gradually opened to the soul. The well-known texts begin to acquire a new and deeper meaning. Familiar expressions convey a knowledge, which the soul wonders never to have before discovered in them. All this new light is directed towards giving a fuller and more perfect comprehension of the mysteries of our faith, which are the mysteries of the life of Jesus" (Leen, *Progress Through Mental Prayer*, p. 29. Sheed & Ward).

Do not read these meditations as a story. Read a few lines slowly; close the book; think about the truth contained in them; apply them to your own life; speak to God about how little you have corresponded to His Will, how anxious you are to do it; listen to God speaking to your soul; make acts of faith, hope, and love to God, and only when that train of thought has been exhausted should you proceed to the next idea. A single Holy Hour will not necessarily require reading a chapter of this book. If one meditates well, a single chapter should provide thoughts for many Holy Hours.

When this book of meditations is exhausted, take up either the Sacred Scriptures or some truly spiritual book, or the life of a saint, and use it for inspiration and for meditation.

✠ J.M.J. ✠

FIRST MEDITATION

THE INCARNATION OF OUR LORD AND SAVIOUR JESUS CHRIST

Love is naturally expansive, but Divine Love is creative. Love told the secret of its goodness to nothingness, and that was creation. Love made something like unto its own image and likeness, and that was man. Love is prodigal of its gifts, and that was the elevation of man to the adoptive sonship of God. Love must always run risks of not being loved in return, for love is free. The human heart refused to return that love in the only way in which love can ever be shown, namely by confidence and trust in a moment of trial. Man thus lost the gifts of God, darkened his intellect, weakened his will, and brought the first or original sin into the world, for sin is ultimately a refusal to love.

It was the refusal of man to love the best that created the most difficult problem in the whole history of humanity, namely the problem of restoring man to the favor of Divine Love. In short, the problem was this: Man had sinned, but his sin was not merely a rebellion against another man, but a revolt against the Infinite Love of God. Therefore his sin was infinite.

Such is one side of the problem. The other side is this: Every infraction or violation of a law demands reparation or atonement. Since God is Infinite Love, He might pardon man and forget the injury, but pardon without compensation would eclipse the Justice, which is the nature of God. Without setting any limits to the Mercy of God, one could understand His action better if His mercy was preceded by a satisfaction for sin, for one can never be merciful unless he is just. Mercy is the overflow of Justice.

But assuming that man should give satisfaction, could he satisfy adequately for his sin? No, because the satisfaction or reparation or atonement, which man had to offer was only finite.

Man, who is finite, owes an infinite debt. But how can a man who owes a million pay the debt with a cent? How can the human atone to the Divine? How can Justice and Mercy be reconciled? If satisfaction is ever to be made for the fall of man, the finite and the infinite, the human and the divine, God and man, must in some way be linked together. It would not do for God alone to come down and suffer as God alone; for then, He would not have anything in common with man; the sin was not God's but man's. It would not do for man alone to suffer or atone, for the merit of his sufferings would be only finite. If the satisfaction were to be complete, two conditions would have to be fulfilled: Man would have to be man to act as man and to atone; man would have to be God in order that his sufferings would have an infinite value. But in order that the finite and the infinite should not be acting as two distinct personalities, and in order that infinite merit should result from man's suffering, God and man in some way would have to become one, or in other words, there would have to be a God-man. If Justice and Mercy were to be reconciled, there would have to be an Incarnation, which means God assuming a human nature in such a way that He would be true God and true man.

There would have to be a union of God and man, and this union took place in the birth of our Lord and Saviour, Jesus Christ.

Love tends to become like the one loved; in fact, it even wishes to become one with the one loved. God loved unworthy man. He willed to become one with him, and that was the Incarnation. One night there went out over the stillness of an evening breeze, out over the white chalk hills of Bethlehem, a cry, a gentle cry. The sea did not hear the cry, for the sea was filled with its own voice. The earth did not hear the cry, for the earth slept. The great men of the earth did not hear the cry, for they could not understand how a child could be greater than a man. The Kings of the earth did not hear the cry, for they could not fathom how a King could be born in a stable. There were only two classes of men who heard the cry that night: Shepherds and Wise Men. Shepherds: those who know they know nothing. Wise Men: those who know they do not know everything. Shepherds: poor simple men who knew only how to tend their flocks, who perhaps could not tell who the Governor of Judea; who, perhaps, did not know a single line of Virgil, though there was not a Roman who could not quote from him was. On the other hand, there were the Wise Men; not Kings, but teachers of Kings; men who knew how to read the stars, to tell the story of their movements; men who were constantly bent on discovery. Both of these heard the cry. The Shepherds found their Shepherd; the Wise Men discovered Wisdom. And the Shepherd and the Wisdom was a Babe in a crib.

He Who is born without a mother in Heaven is born without a father on earth. He Who made His mother is born of His mother. He Who made all flesh is born of flesh. "The bird that built the nest is hatched therein." Maker of the sun, under the sun; Molder of the earth, on the earth; Ineffably Wise, a little infant; filling the world, lying in a manger; ruling the stars, suckling a breast; the mirth of Heaven weeps, God becomes man; Creator, a creature. Rich becomes poor; Divinity, incarnate; Majesty, subjugated; Liberty, captive; Eternity, time; Master, a servant; Truth, accused; Judge, judged; Justice, condemned; Lord, scourged; Power, bound with ropes; King, crowned with thorns; Salvation, wounded; Life, dead. "The Eternal Word is dumb." Marvel of marvels! Union of unions! Three mysterious unions in one; Divinity and humanity; Virginity and fecundity; Faith and the heart of man.

It takes a Divine, an Infinite Being to use the very instruments of defeat as the instruments of victory. The fall came through three realities: First, a disobedient man: Adam. Second, a proud woman: Eve. Third, a tree. The reconciliation and redemption of man came through these same three. For the disobedient man, Adam, was the obedient new Adam of the human race, Christ; for the proud Eve, there was the humble Mary; and for the tree, the Cross.

Our Lord did not walk about the earth forever, telling people platitudes about truth. He was not just explaining truth, defeat, resignation, and sacrifice. Everyone else did this. The goal He was seeking was death. From the beginning to the end, only one vision was before His eyes – He was going to die. Not die because He could not help it, but die because He willed it. Death was not an incident in His career; it was not an accident in His plan – it was the one business He had to do. All during His redeeming life, He looked forward to His redemptive death. He anticipated His blood-shedding on Calvary by His circumcision at eight days of age. At the beginning of His public ministry, His presence inspired John to cry out to his disciples at the Jordan: "Behold the Lamb of God" (John 1:29). He answered to the confession of His Divinity by Peter at Caesarea-Philippi that He "must suffer many things from the elders and scribes and chief priests, and be put to death, and on the third day rise again" (Matt. 16:21); the leaden weighted days caused Him to cry out in beautiful impatience: "I have a baptism to be baptized with; and how distressed I am until it is accomplished!" (Luke 12:50). To the member of the Sanhedrin who would seek a sign, He foretold His death on the Cross. He answered: "And as Moses lifted up the serpent in the desert, even so, must the Son of Man be lifted up, that those who believe in him may not perish, but may have life everlasting" (John 3:14-15). To the Pharisees, who were as sheep without a shepherd, He spoke: "I am the good shepherd. The good shepherd lays down his life for his sheep . . . and I lay down my life for my sheep . . . No one takes it from me, but I lay it down of myself. I have power to lay it down, and I have power to take it up again. Such is the command I have received from my Father" (John 10:11, 16, 18). To all men of all times who would

27

forget that He is come as Our Redeemer and Saviour, He speaks the most tender words that were ever caught up on this sinful earth: "For God so loved the world that he gave his only-begotten Son, that those who believe in him may not perish, but may have life everlasting. For God did not send his Son into the world in order to judge the world, but that the world might be saved through him" (John 3:16-17).

The Repentance and Confession of David After His Sin

Have mercy on me, O God, according to thy great mercy. And according to the multitude of thy tender mercies blot out my iniquity. Wash me yet more from my iniquity and cleanse me from my sin. For I know my iniquity, and my sin is always before me. To thee only have I sinned, and have done evil before thee: that thou mayst be justified in thy words, and mayst overcome when thou art judged. For behold, I was conceived in iniquities, and in sins did my mother conceive me. For behold, thou hast loved truth: the uncertain and hidden things of thy wisdom thou hast made manifest to me. Thou shalt sprinkle me with hyssop, and I shall be cleansed: though shalt wash me, and I shall be made whiter than snow. To my hearing thou shalt give joy and gladness: and the bones that have been humbled shall rejoice. Turn away thy face from my sins, and blot out all my iniquities. Create a clean heart in me, O God: and renew a right spirit within my bowels. Cast me not away from thy face, and take not thy holy spirit from me. Restore unto me the joy of thy salvation, and strengthen me with a perfect spirit. I will teach the unjust thy ways: and the wicked shall be converted to thee. Deliver me from blood, O God, thou God of my salvation: and my tongue shall extol thy justice. O Lord, thou wilt open my lips: and my mouth shall declare thy praise. For if thou hadst desired sacrifice, I would indeed have given it: with burnt offerings, thou wilt not be delighted. A sacrifice to God is an afflicted spirit: a contrite and humbled heart, O God, thou wilt not despise. Deal favorably, O Lord, in thy good will with Sion; that the walls of Jerusalem may be built up. Then shalt thou accept the sacrifice of justice, oblations, and whole burnt offerings: then shall they lay calves upon thy altar" (Ps. 50:3 - 21).

Prayer of St. Augustine

(From The Raccolta)

"Lord Jesus, may I know myself and know Thee. And desire nothing save only Thee. May I hate myself and love Thee. May I do everything for the sake of Thee. May I humble myself and exalt Thee. May I think of nothing except Thee. May I die to myself and live in Thee. May I receive whatever happens as from Thee. May I banish self and follow Thee. And ever desire to follow Thee. May I fly from myself and fly to Thee, that I may deserve to be defended by Thee. May I fear for myself and fear Thee, and be among those who are chosen by Thee. May I distrust myself and trust in Thee. May I be willing to obey on account of Thee. May I cling to nothing but to Thee. May I be poor for the sake of Thee. Look upon me that I may love Thee. Call me that I may see Thee, and ever and ever enjoy Thee. Amen."

✠ J.M.J. ✠

SECOND MEDITATION

HOW CHRIST LIVES
IN US TODAY

How often we hear souls bemoan that they are so distant from Galilee and so removed from Jesus. The world is full of men and women who think of Our Lord solely and uniquely in terms of what their eyes can see, their ears can hear, and their hands can touch. How many there are who, starting with the truth that He was a great Teacher of commanding influence Who walked the earth 2,000 years ago, gather up the details of the scenery of the lake and hill country of Galilee, and use their imagination better to portray the exact circumstances of His earthly life; but here the appreciation of His life ends. They have learned habitually to think of Him as someone who belongs to human history, like Caesar, Washington, or Mohammed; they think of Him as one who lived on earth and passed away.

But where He is, what His nature is, whether He can act upon us now, whether He can hear us, be approached by us, are thoughts which are contemptuously dismissed as belonging to the category of theological abstractions and foolish dogmas. These very souls may follow His example in such and such an instance, apply His Beatitudes to this or that circumstance of their life, look upon His life as a great sacrifice and inspiration; but beyond that Christ means nothing to them. He is the greatest man who ever lived, but He is nothing more. They indeed are among those of whom St. Paul said that they know Christ only according to the flesh.

It must be admitted that the continued sensible and visible presence of Our Saviour would have been a continuous inspiration to our lives, but we must not forget that He Himself said the night before He died: "It is expedient for you that I depart" (John 16:7). Strange words, these. Why should they be spoken at a moment when He had weaned the hearts of His Apostles away from their nets, boats, and custom tables, and had entwined them so closely about His own Sacred Heart? How could it be expedient for them that He go? It was expedient for Him to go in order that He might be nearer to us. This is the very reason He gave for His going: "For if I do not go, the Advocate will not come to you; but if I go, I will send him to you . . . a little while and you shall see me no longer; and again a little while, and you shall see me because I go to the Father . . . I will see you again, and your heart shall rejoice; and your joy no one shall take from you" (John 16:7-8, 16, 22).

In these solemn words spoken on the eve of His crucifixion, He explicitly stated that He was going back to the boundless depths of His Father's Life whence He came, but His going would not leave them orphans, for He would come again in a new way; namely, by His Spirit. Our Lord was here equivalently saying that if He remained on earth in His physical life, He would have been only an example to be copied; but if He went to His Father and sent His Spirit, then He would be a life to be lived. If he remained on earth He would always have been outside us, external to us; an external Voice, an external Life, an eternal Example – He could never be possessed other than by an embrace.

But once He ascended into heaven and sat at the right hand of the Father in the Glory which is His, then He could send His Spirit into our souls, so that He would be with us not as an external Person, but as a living Soul; then He would be not just a mere something mechanical to be copied, but a something vital to be reproduced, not a something external to be portrayed in our lives, but a something living to be developed within us. His ascension into Heaven, and His sending of His Spirit, alone make it possible for Him to unite Himself wholly with us, to take up His abode with us, body and blood, soul and divinity, and to be in the strictest sense of the term "Christ in us." It was expedient, therefore, that He go. Otherwise, He would have belonged to history and to a country. Now He belongs to men.

Thanks to His Invisible Spirit, which He sends into His Mystical Body, Christ is living now on earth just as really and truly as He was living in Galilee twenty centuries ago. In a certain sense He is closer to us now than then, for His very body then made Him external to us, but thanks to His Spirit, He can now live in us as the very Soul of our soul, the very Spirit of our spirit, the Truth of our mind, the Love of our heart, and the Desire of our will. Thus the life of Christ is transferred by the Spirit from the region of purely historical studies, which we investigate with our reason, to the realm of spiritual experience, where He speaks directly to our soul. It may have been a great consolation for the Canaanite woman to have touched the hem of His garment, for Magdalen to have kissed His feet, for John to have leaned on His breast the night of the Last Supper, but all these intimacies are external. They have great force and appeal because they are sensible, but none of them can even vaguely approximate the union, the intimacy, which comes of possessing Christ inwardly, thanks to His Holy Spirit. The greatest joys of life are those which come from unity. We never reach the height of unity until there is a fusion of loves, of thoughts, and of desires, a unity so profound that we think with the one we love, love with the one we love, desire what he desires; and this unity is found in its perfection when the soul is made one with the Spirit of Christ which is the Spirit of God. The joys that come from human friendships, even the noblest, are but the shadows and fond reflections of the joy of a soul possessed of the Spirit of Christ. Elevate human happiness, which comes from union with the one loved, to the extremest point the heart can endure, and even that is but a spark compared to the Great Flame of the Spirit of Christ burning in a soul that loves Him.

What precisely is this life of Christ in the baptized soul? It is grace, a supernatural gift bestowed on us through the merits of Jesus Christ for our salvation.

The whole order of creation affords us an analogy of the gift-quality of grace. If a stone, say the rock of Gibraltar, should suddenly break out into bloom, it would be something transcending its nature. If a rose one day would become conscious, and see and feel and touch, it would be a supranatural act – an act totally undue to the nature of the rose as such. If an animal would break out into a reasoning process and speak words of wisdom, it would be a supranatural act, for it is not in the nature of an animal to be rational. So too, but in a far more rigorous manner, if man, who by nature is a creature of God, becomes a child of God, a member of the family of the Trinity, and a brother of Jesus Christ, it is a supernatural act for man, and a gift which surpasses all the exigencies and powers of his nature, even more than blooming surpasses the nature and powers of marble.

Grace makes man a "new creature," infinitely higher than his former condition, more than an animal would be if it spoke with the wisdom of Socrates. There is nothing in all creation like that gift by which God calls man a son, and man calls God "Father." The difference between mere human life and human life rendered deiform by grace is not one of development but of generation. The source of life in both cases is as different as human and Divine Paternity. The distance, which separates some minerals from the vegetable kingdom, may be only a hair's breadth – but the distance which separates human life and Divine Life is infinite. "No one can pass from thence hence."

The world, in the eyes of God, is divided into two classes, the sons of men and the sons of God. All are called to be sons of God, but not all accept the gift worthily, believing that if they should take Christ as their portion, they would have naught else besides. It is to forget that the whole contains the parts and that in Perfect Life, we have the joys of finite life in an infinite degree. Both types of sons are born, the one according to the flesh, the other according to the spirit. "That which is born of the flesh is flesh; and that which is born of the Spirit is spirit" (John 3: 6). Being born of the flesh incorporates us into the life of Adam; being born of the spirit – of waters of the Holy Spirit – incorporates us into the Life of Christ. The sons of God are twice-born; the sons of men once born. There is more difference between two souls on this earth, one in the state of grace and the other not in that state, than there is between two souls, one in the state of grace in this life and the other enjoying the eternal blessedness of Heaven. The reason is that grace is the germ of glory, and some day will blossom into glory just as the acorn someday will become the oak. But the soul not possessed with grace has no such potencies in it. "Beloved," says St. John, "now we are the children of God, and it has not yet appeared what we shall be. We know that, when he appears, we shall be like to him, for we shall see him just as he is" (1 John 3:2).

✠ J.M.J. ✠

The Different Effects of Nature and Grace

(Thomas à Kempis, *Imitation of Christ,*
Book III, Chapter 54)

"Son observe diligently the motions of *nature* and *grace*; for they move very opposite ways, and very subtly, and can hardly be distinguished but by a spiritual man, and one that is internally illuminated.

"All men, indeed, aim at good, and pretend to something of good in what they do and say: therefore, under the appearance of good, many are deceived.

"*Nature* is crafty, and draws away many; ensnares them, and deceives them, and always intends herself for her end:

"But *grace* walks with simplicity, turns away from all appearance of evil, offers no deceits, and does all things purely for God, in whom also she rests as in her last end.

"*Nature* is unwilling to be mortified, or to be restrained, or to be overcome, or to be subject; neither will she of her own accord be brought under:

"But *grace* studies the mortification of her own self, resists sensuality, seeks to be subject, covets to be overcome, aims not at following her own liberty, loves to be kept under discipline, and desires not to have the command over any one; but under God ever to live, stand, and be; and for God's sake is ever ready humbly to bow down herself under all human creatures.

"*Nature* labors for her own interest, and thinks what gain she may reap from others:

"But *grace* considers not what may be advantageous and profitable to herself but rather what may be profitable to many.

"*Nature* willingly receives honor and respect:

"But *grace* faithfully attributes all honor and glory to God.

"*Nature* is afraid of being put to shame and despised:

"But *grace* is glad to suffer reproach for the name of Jesus.

"*Nature* loves idleness and bodily rest:

"But *grace* cannot be idle, and willingly embraces labor.

"*Nature* seeks to have things that are curious and fine, and does not care for things that are cheap and coarse:

"But *grace* is pleased with that which is plain and humble, rejects not coarse things, nor refuses to be clad in old clothes.

"*Nature* has regard to temporal things, rejoices at earthly gain, is troubled at losses, and is provoked at every slight, injurious word:

"But *grace* attends to things eternal, and cleaves not to those which pass with time; neither is she disturbed at the loss of things, nor exasperated with hard words, for she places her

43

treasure and her joy in heaven, where nothing is
lost.

"*Nature* is covetous, and is more willing to
take than to give, and loves to have things to
herself.

"But *grace* is bountiful and openhearted,
avoids selfishness, is contented with little and
judges it more happy to give than to receive.

"*Nature* inclines to creatures, to her own
flesh, to vanities, and to gadding abroad:

"But *grace* draws to God and to virtue,
renounces creatures, flies the world, hates the
desires of the flesh, restrains wandering about,
and is ashamed to appear in public.

"*Nature* willingly receives exterior comfort,
in which she may be sensibly delighted:

"But *grace* seeks to be comforted in God
alone, and beyond all things visible, to be
delighted in the Sovereign Good.

"*Nature* does all for her own lucre and interest; she can do nothing gratis, but hopes to gain something equal or better, or praise, or favor for her good deeds, and covets to have her actions and gifts much valued:

"But *grace* seeks nothing temporal, nor requires any other recompense but God alone for her reward, nor desires anything more of the necessaries of this life that may be serviceable for the obtaining a happy eternity.

"*Nature* rejoices in a multitude of friends and kindred; she glories in the nobility of her stock and descent; she fawns on them that are in power, flatters the rich, and applauds such as are like herself:

"But *grace* loves even her enemies, and is not puffed up with having a great many friends, nor has any value for family or birth, unless when joined to greater virtue, she rather favors the poor than the rich; she has more compassion for the innocent than the powerful; she rejoices with him that loves the truth, and not with the deceitful; she ever exhorts the good to be zealous for better

45

gifts, and to become like to the Son of God by the exercise of virtues.

"*Nature* easily complains of want and of trouble:

"But *grace* bears poverty with constancy.

"*Nature* turns all things to herself, and for herself, she labors and disputes:

"But *grace* refers all things to God, from whom all originally proceed; she attributes no good to herself, nor does she arrogantly presume of herself: she does not contend, nor prefer her own opinion to others, but in every sense and understanding she submits herself to the eternal wisdom and the divine examination.

"*Nature* covets to know secrets, and to hear news; is willing to appear abroad, and to have experience of many things by the senses; desires to be taken notice of, and to do such things as may procure praise and admiration:

"But *grace* cares not for the hearing of news and curious things, because all this springs from the old corruption since nothing is new or lasting upon earth.

"She teaches, therefore, to restrain the senses, to avoid vain complacency and ostentation, humbly to hide those things which are worthy of praise and admiration, and from everything, and in every knowledge, to seek the fruit of spiritual profit, and the praise and honor of God.

"She desires not to have herself for what belongs to her extolled; but wishes that God may be blessed in his gifts, who bestows all through mere love.

"This *grace* is a supernatural light, and a certain special gift of God, and the proper mark of the elect, and the pledge of eternal salvation, which elevates a man from things of the earth to the love of heavenly things, and, if carnal, makes him spiritual.

"Wherefore, by how much the more nature is kept down and subdued, with so much the greater abundance *grace* is infused, and the inward man, by new visitations, is daily more reformed according to the image of God."

✠ J.M.J. ✠

48

THIRD MEDITATION

HOW THAT DIVINE LIFE IS LOST AND OUR FINAL END

Sin is the killing of the Christ-life in our soul. Our conscience is the courtroom of Pilate. Daily and hourly there are brought before us Barabbas and Christ. Barabbas comes as vice, murder, blasphemy – Christ comes as virtue, love, and purity. Which of the two shall be released?

If we die in the state of sin, we shall be judged as sinners. What is Judgment? Judgment may be considered both from God's point of view and from our point of view.

From God's point of view, Judgment is a recognition. Two souls appear before the sight of God in that split-second after death. One is in the state of grace; the other is not. The Judge looks into the soul in the state of grace. He sees there a resemblance to His nature, for grace is a participation in Divine Nature. Just as a mother knows her child because of the resemblance of nature, so too, God knows His own children by resemblance of nature. If they are born of Him, He knows it. Seeing in that soul, His likeness, the Sovereign Judge, Our Lord, and Saviour Jesus Christ says in effect: "Come, ye blessed of My Father. I have taught you to pray, 'Our Father.' I am the natural Son; you, the adopted son. Come into the Kingdom I have prepared for you from all eternity."

The other soul, not possessing the family traits and likeness of the Trinity, meets an entirely different reception from the Judge. As a mother knows her neighbor's son is not her own, because there is no participation in nature, so too, Jesus Christ, seeing in the sinful soul no participation of His nature, can only say those words which signify non-recognition, "I know you not"; and it is a terrible thing not to be known by God!

It is not wise to presume on God's mercy.
9/16/24

Such is Judgment from the Divine point of view. From the human point of view, it is also a recognition, but a recognition of unfitness or fitness. A very distinguished visitor is announced at the door, but I am in my working clothes, my hands and face are dirty. I am in no condition to present myself before such an august personage, and I refuse to see him until I can improve my appearance. A soul stained with sin acts very much the same when it goes before the judgment seat of God. It sees, on one hand, His Majesty, His Purity, His Brilliance, and on the other its own baseness, its sinfulness, and its unworthiness. It does not entreat or argue, it does not plead a case – it sees; and from out of the depths comes its own judgment, "Oh, Lord, I am not worthy." The soul that is stained with venial sins casts itself into purgatory to wash its baptismal robes, but the soul irremediably stained – the soul dead to Divine Life – casts itself into Hell just as naturally as a stone, which is released from my hand, falls to the ground.

But is there a Hell? The modern world no longer believes in it. True it is that many of our present-day prophets deny Hell, and that makes us ask the reason of the denial. The reason is probably psychological. There are two possible orientations for a man. Either he must adapt his life to dogmas, or he must adapt dogmas to his life. "If we do not live as we think, we soon begin to think as we live." If our life is not regulated in accordance with the Gospel, then the thought of Hell is a very uncomfortable kind of thought. To ease my conscience, I must deny it. I must suit a dogma to my mode of life. And this is borne out by experience. Some believe in Hell, fear it, hate it, and avoid sin. Others love sin, deny Hell, but always fear it.

But granted that such be the reason for its denial, these same prophets will ask, how do you know there is a Hell? Very clearly, because Jesus Christ said there was. Either there is a Hell, or Infinite Truth is a liar. I cannot accept the second proposition, so I must accept the first.

Heaven and Hell are not mere afterthoughts in the actual Divine Plan. God did not, by a second act of His Will and Omnipotence, create Heaven and Hell to reward and punish those who obey or disobey His Divine Law. They are not arbitrary decrees; mere things to patch up an original plan disturbed by sin. No law can exist without sanction. If there were no Hell in the present order of salvation, what would be the consequence? It would mean that whatever evil we did, and regardless of how long we did it, and the hatred with which we did it, God would all the while be indifferent to our moral acts; which would be another way of saying that Law is indifferent to lawlessness.

All our misconceptions concerning Heaven and Hell are founded on our inability to see how they are bound up necessarily with our acts in the moral order. There are many who regard Heaven only as an arbitrary reward for a good life, a kind of token in appreciation of our victory, as a silver loving cup is awarded to the winner of a race. Such is not the whole truth. Heaven is not related to a good Christian life in the same way a silver cup is related to the winning of a race, for the silver cup may or may not follow the victory; it is not something inseparably bound up with it – something else might be given or perhaps nothing at all. Rather, Heaven is related to a Christian life as learning is related to study; that is why theologians call grace the "seed of glory." If I study, I acquire knowledge by that very act; the two are inseparable, one being the fruition of the other. And in this connection it is well to remember that Heaven in the present constitution of God's world is not merely a reward, it is in a certain sense, a "right," the right of heirs – for we are heirs of the Kingdom of Heaven in virtue of the gift of Divine Adoption into the sonship of God by a Heavenly Father.

Hell, too, is often explained too exclusively in terms of arbitrariness. It is made to appear as a kind of punishment wholly unrelated to a life of sin and the abandonment of the gift of God. Hell is not related to an evil life as a spanking is related to an act of disobedience, for such a punishment need not necessarily follow the act. Rather Hell is bound up with an evil life in precisely the same way as blindness is related to the plucking out of an eye. If I lose my eye, I am blind necessarily, and if I rebel against God, refuse His pardon, and die in sin, I must suffer Hell as a consequence. There is equity in human law, and there is equity in the Divine Law. A sin involves first a turning away from God, second, a turning to creatures. Because of the first element, the sinner suffers the Pain of Loss or the deprivation of the Beatific Vision. Because of the turning to creatures, the sinner suffers the Pain of Sense, which is a punishment by created things for the abuse of created things, and this is commonly referred to as "hell fire." The difference between the Pain of Loss and the Pain of Sense consists in that the former is caused by the absence of something, the latter by the presence of something. Of the two pains the first is the more terrible, for it is the final and never-ceasing frustration of the craving of an immortal being; it is the missing of the goal of life; it is the having failed so utterly as never to admit of another start; it is to want God and yet hate oneself for wanting Him; it is an asking never to receive, a seeking never to find, a knocking at a gate eternally closed; it is, above all, a void created by the absence of the Life, the Truth, and Love which the soul eternally craves. How eagerly souls yearn for life; how tenaciously they cling to even a straw to save from drowning! How they desire to prolong life even into eternity! What must it be then to miss, not a long human life, but the very Life of all Living! It is a kind of living death, like the waking up in a sepulcher. Truth, too, is the desire of souls. Knowledge is a passion, and the human deprival of it is pain, as is so forcibly brought home to us when we are deprived of the knowledge of a secret in which others share.

What must it be then to be deprived not of an earthly truth, not something which we could learn later on perhaps, but the Truth outside of which there is no truth or knowledge or wisdom at all? It would be worse than earthly life without sun or moon, a kind of cavernous darkness in which one moves about knowing that one might have known the light of truth but would not. Finally, how dull an earthly life would be without the affection or the love of parents, brothers, sisters, and friends! How heavy our hearts would be if every other heart turned to stone! Then what must it be to be deprived of Love without which there is no love? It is to have one's heart stolen and still be able to live without it.

Heaven and Hell are the natural and inseparable results of acts good and bad in the supernatural order. This life is the springtime; judgment is the harvest. "For what things a man shall sow, those also shall he reap. For he that soweth in his flesh, of the flesh also shall reap corruption. But he that soweth in the spirit shall reap life everlasting."

Why do souls go to Hell? In the last analysis, souls go to Hell for one great reason, and that is – they refuse to love. Love pardons everything except one thing – refusal to love. A young man loves a maiden. He makes it known his affection toward her, showers her with gifts, bestows on her more than the ordinary share of the courtesies of life, but his love is repulsed. Keeping it pure, he pursues, but all in vain; she turns a deaf ear to his wooing. Love, so long denied and cast aside, suddenly reaches a point where it will cry out: "All right, love can do no more, I am through now; we are finished." It has reached the point of abandonment.

God is the Divine Lover. As the Hound of Heaven, He is continually in pursuit of souls. Way back in the agelessness of eternity, He loved us with an Eternal Love. When time begins for an individual soul, He gives it the riches of nature, calls it to be an adopted son, feeds it on His own substance and makes it an heir of Heaven. But that soul may soon forget such goodness, and yet God does not forget to love. He pursues the soul, sends discontent deep into it to bring it back to Him, cuts purposely across its path to manifest His presence, send His ambassadors to it, lavishes it with medicinal graces; and still, Divine Love is spurned. Finally rejected more often than seventy times seven, Divine Love abandons the pursuit of such a soul which turns from Him at the end of its lease on life and cries out: "It is finished. Love can do no more." And it is a terrible thing not to be loved, and most of all not to be loved by Love. That is Hell. Hell is a place where there is no love.

On Considering One's Death

(Thomas à Kempis, *Imitation of Christ,*
Book 1, Chapter 23)

"Very quickly, your life here will end; consider then, what may be in store for you elsewhere.

"A man is here today, and tomorrow he is vanished. And when he is taken away from sight, he is quickly also out of mind.

"Oh! the dullness and hardness of man's heart, which only thinks on what is present, and looks not forward to things to come.

"Therefore, in every deed and every thought, act as though you were to die this very day. If you had a good conscience, you would not fear death very much.

"It were better for you to avoid sin than to be afraid of death.

"If you are not prepared today, how will you be prepared tomorrow?·

"Tomorrow is an uncertain day; and how do you know you will be alive tomorrow?

"What benefit is it to live long, when we advance so little?

"Ah! long life does not always make us better, but often adds to our guilt.

"Would to God we had behaved ourselves well in this world, even for one day!

"Many count the years of their conversion, but oftentimes the fruit of amendment is small. "If it be frightful to die, perhaps it will be more dangerous to live longer.

"Blessed is he that has always the hour of his death before his eyes, and every day disposes himself to die.

"If you have ever seen a man die, remember that you too must also pass the same way. "In the morning, imagine that you may not live until night; and when evening comes, presume not to promise yourself the next morning.

"Be always ready and live in such manner that death may never find you unprovided.

"Many die suddenly, and when they little think of it: *For the Son of Man will come at the hour when he is not looked for* (Matt. 24: 44). When that last hour shall come, then you will begin to have quite other thoughts of your whole past life; and you will be exceedingly grieved that you have been so negligent and remiss.

"How happy and prudent is he who strives to be such now in this life, as he desires to be found at his death.

"For it will give a man a great confidence of dying happily if he has a perfect contempt of the world, a fervent desire of advancing in virtue, a love for discipline, the spirit of penance, a ready obedience, self-denial, and patience in bearing all adversities for the love of Christ.

"You can do many good things when in good health; but when you are sick, I know not what you will be able to do.

"Few are improved by sickness; they also that travel much abroad seldom become holy.

"Trust not in your friends and relatives, and do not put off the care of your soul till later; for who will care when you are gone?

"It is better now to provide in time and send some good ahead of you than to trust others helping you after your death.

"If you do not care for your own welfare now, who will care when you are gone?

"The present time is very precious. *Behold now is the acceptable time; behold, now is the day of salvation* (2 Cor. 6:2).

"But it is greatly to be lamented, that you do not spend this time more profitably, where you might purchase everlasting life in a better way! The time will come when you will wish for one day or hour to amend, and I know not whether you will obtain it.

"O my dearly beloved, from how great a danger which you can free yourself; from how great a fear may you be freed, if you will but now be always fearful, and looking for death!

"Strive now so to live, that in the hour of your death you will rather rejoice than fear.

"Learn now to despise all things, that then you will begin to live with Christ. Learn now to die to the world, that then you may freely go to Christ.

"Chastise your body now by penance, that you may then have an assured confidence." Ah, fool! Why do you think to live long, when you are not sure of one day?

"How many, thinking to live long, have been deceived, and unexpectedly have been snatched away.

"How often have you heard related, that such a one was slain by sword; another drowned; another, falling from on high, broke his neck; this man died at the table; that other came to his end when he was at play?

"Some have perished by fire; some by the sword; some by pestilence; and some by robbers.

"Thus, death is the end of all, and man's life pass suddenly like a shadow.
"Who will remember you when you are dead, and who will pray for you?

"Do now, beloved, do now all you can, because you know not when you shall die, nor what fate will be after death.

"Gather for yourself the riches of immortality while you have time; think of nothing but your salvation; care for nothing but the things of God.

"Make friends for yourself now, by honoring the saints of God, by imitating their actions so that when you shall depart from this life, they may receive you into everlasting dwellings.

"Keep yourself as a pilgrim, and a stranger upon earth, to whom the affairs of this world do not in the least belong.

"Keep your heart free, and raised upwards to God, because you have not here a lasting home.

"To Him direct your daily prayers, with sighs and tears; that after death, your spirit may be worthy to pass happily to our Lord. Amen."

✠ J.M.J. ✠

FOURTH MEDITATION

THE DUTY OF SELF-DENIAL

(St. John Henry Newman, *Parochial and Plain Sermons,* Vol. 7, Sermon 7)

Self-Denial of some kind or other is involved, as is evident, in the very notion of renewal and holy obedience. To change our hearts is to learn to love things which we do not naturally love – to unlearn the love of this world; but this involves, of course, a thwarting of our natural wishes and tastes. To be righteous and obedient implies self-command, but to possess power, we must have gained it; nor can we gain it without a vigorous struggle, a persevering warfare against ourselves. The very notion of being religious implies self-denial because, by nature, we do not love religion."

"... it is our duty, not only to deny ourselves in what is sinful but even in a certain measure, in lawful things, to keep a restraint over ourselves even in innocent pleasures and enjoyments."

"... Fasting is clearly a Christian duty, as our Saviour implies in His Sermon on the Mount. Now, what is fasting but in refraining from what is lawful; not merely from what is sinful, but what is innocent? – From that bread which we might lawfully take and eat with thanksgiving, but which at certain times we do not take, in order to deny ourselves. Such as Christian self-denial – not merely a mortification of what is sinful, but an abstinence even from God's blessings.

"Again consider the following declaration of our Saviour: He first tells us, 'How narrow the gate and close the way that leads to life! And few, there are who find it' (Matt. 7:14). And again: 'Strive to enter by the narrow gate; for many, I tell you, will seek to enter and will not be able' (Luke 13:24). Then he explains to us what this peculiar difficulty of a Christian's life consists in: 'If anyone comes to me and does not hate his father and mother, and wife and children, and brothers and sisters, yes, and even his own life, he cannot be my disciple' (Luke 14:26). Now whatever is precisely meant by this (which I will not stop here to inquire), so far is evident, that our Lord enjoins a certain refraining, not merely from sin, but from innocent comforts and enjoyments of this life, or a self-denial in things lawful.

"Again, He says, 'If anyone wishes to come after me, let him deny himself, and take up his cross daily, and follow me' (Luke 9:23). Here he shows us from His own example what Christian self-denial is. It is taking on us a cross after His pattern, not a mere refraining from sin, for He had no sin, but a giving up what we might lawfully use. This was the peculiar character in which Christ came on earth. It was this spontaneous and exuberant self-denial, which brought Him down. He who was one with God, took upon Him our nature, and suffered death – and why? to save us whom He needed not save. Thus He denied Himself and took up His cross. This is the very aspect, in which God, as revealed in Scripture, is distinguished from that exhibition of His glory, which nature gives us: power, wisdom, love, mercy, long-suffering – these attributes, though far more fully and clearly displayed in Scripture than in nature, still are in their degree seen on the face of the visible creation; but self-denial, if it may be said, this incomprehensible attribute of Divine Providence, is disclosed to us only in Scripture. 'For God so loved the world that He gave his only-begotten Son' (John 3:16). Here is self-denial. And the Son of God so loved you, that 'being rich, he became poor for your sakes' (2 Cor. 8:9). Here is our Saviour's self-denial. 'He pleased not Himself.'"

"Such is Christian self-denial, and it is incumbent upon us for many reasons. The Christian denies himself in things lawful because he is aware of his own weakness and liability to sin; he dares not walk on the edge of a precipice; instead of going to the extreme of what is allowable, he keeps at a distance from evil, that he may be safe. He abstains lest he should not be temperate: he fasts lest he should eat and drink with the drunken. As is evident, many things are in themselves right and unexceptionable which are inexpedient in the case of a weak and sinful creature; his case is like that of a sick person; many kinds of food, good for a man in health, are hurtful when he is ill – wine is poison to a man in a fierce fever. And just so, many acts, thoughts, and feelings, which would have been allowable in Adam before his fall, are prejudicial or dangerous in man fallen. For instance, anger is not sinful in itself. St. Paul implies this, when he says, 'Be angry and do not sin' (Eph. 4:26). And our Saviour on one occasion is said to have been angry, and He was sinless. Almighty God, too, is angry with the wicked. Anger, then, is not in itself a sinful feeling; but in man, constituted as he is, it is so highly dangerous to indulge it, that self-denial here is a duty from mere prudence. It is almost impossible for a man to be angry only so far as he ought to be; he will exceed the right limit; his anger will degenerate into pride, sullenness, malice, cruelty, revenge, and hatred. It will inflame his diseased soul and poison it. Therefore, he must abstain from it, as if it were in itself a sin (though it is not), for it is practically such to him."

"If we have good health, and are in easy circumstances, let us beware of high-mindedness, self-sufficiency, self-conceit, arrogance; of delicacy of living, indulgences, luxuries, comforts. Nothing is so likely to corrupt our hearts, and to seduce us from God, as to surround ourselves with comforts – to have things our own way – to be center of a sort of world, whether of things animate or inanimate, which minister to us. For then, in turn, we shall depend on them; they will become necessary to us; their very service and adulation will lead us to trust ourselves to them, and to idolize them. What examples are there in Scripture of soft luxurious men! Was it Abraham before the Law, who wandered through his days, without a home? or Moses, who gave the Law, and died in the wilderness? or David under the Law, who 'had no proud looks,' and was 'as a weaned child'? or the Prophets, in the latter days of the Law, who wandered in sheep-skins and goat-skins? or the Baptist, when the Gospel was superseding it, who was clad in raiment of camel's hair and ate the food of the wilderness? or the Apostles who were 'the offscouring of all things'? or our blessed Saviour, who 'had not a place to lay His head'? Who are the soft luxurious men in Scripture? There was the rich man, who 'fared sumptuously every day,' and then 'lifted up his eyes in hell, being in torments.' There was that other, whose 'ground brought forth plentifully,' and who said, 'Soul, thou hast much goods laid up for many years'; and his soul was required of him that night. There was Demas, who forsook St. Paul, 'having loved this present world'! And, alas! There was that highly-favored, that divinely-inspired king, rich and wise Solomon, whom it availed nothing to have measured the earth and numbered its inhabitants, when in his old age he 'loved many strange women,' and worshipped their gods."

"You need not attempt to draw any precise line between what is sinful and what is only allowable: look up to Christ and deny yourselves everything, whatever its character, which you think He would have you relinquish. You need not calculate and measure if you love much: you need not perplex yourselves with points of curiosity if you have a heart to venture after Him. True, difficulties will sometimes arise, but they will seldom be. He bids you take up your cross; therefore accept the daily opportunities which occur of yielding to others, when you need not yield, and of doing unpleasant services, which you might avoid. He bids those who would be highest, live as the lowest: therefore, turn from ambitious thoughts, and (as far as you religiously may) make resolves against taking on your authority and rule. He bids you sell and give alms; therefore, hate to spend money on yourself. Shut your eyes to praise, when it grows loud: set your face like a flint, when the world ridicules, and smile at its threats. Learn to master your heart, when it would burst forth into vehemence, or prolong a barren sorrow, or dissolve into unseasonable tenderness. Curb your tongue, and turn away your eye, lest you fall into temptation. Avoid the dangerous air which relaxes you, and brace yourself upon the heights. Be up at prayer 'a great while before day,' and seek the true, your only Bridegroom, 'by night on your bed.' So shall self-denial become natural to you, and a change come over you, gently and imperceptibly; and, like Jacob, you will lie down in the waste, and you will soon see Angels, and a way opened for you into heaven."

On Judgment and the Punishment of Sinners

(Thomas à Kempis, *Imitation of Christ,*
Book 1, Chapter 24)

"In all things look to the end, and how you shall be able to stand before a severe judge, from whom nothing is hidden; who takes no bribes, nor receives excuses, but will judge that which is just.

"O most wretched and foolish sinner, what answer will you make to God, who knows all your sins; you who sometimes are afraid of the looks of an angry man?

"Why do you not provide for yourself against the day of judgment, when no man can be excused or defended by another, but everyone shall have enough to do to answer for himself?

"At present, your labor is profitable, your tears are acceptable, your sighs will be heard, and your sorrow is satisfactory, and may purge away your sins.

"A patient man has a great and wholesome purgatory, who, receiving injuries, is more concerned at another person's sin than his own wrong; who willingly prays for his adversaries, and from his heart forgives offences; who delays not to ask forgiveness of others; who is easier moved to compassion than to anger; who frequently uses violence to himself, and labours to bring the flesh wholly under subjection to the spirit.

"It is better now to purge away our sins and root out vices than to reserve them to be purged hereafter.

"Truly, we deceive ourselves through the inordinate love we bear to our flesh.

"What other things shall that fire feed on but your sins?

"The more you spare yourself now, and follow the flesh, the more grievously shall you suffer hereafter, and the more fuel you will lay up for that fire.

"In what things a man has more sinned, in those shall he be more heavily punished?

"There, the slothful will be pricked forward with burning goads, and the glutton will be tormented with extreme hunger and thirst.

"There the luxurious and the lovers of pleasure will be covered all over with burning pitch and stinking brimstone; and the envious, like mad dogs, will howl for grief.

78

"There is no vice which will not there have its proper torment.

"There, the proud will be filled with all confusion, and the covetous be straitened with most miserable want.

"There one hour of suffering will be more sharp than a hundred years here spent in the most rigid penance.

"There is no rest, no comfort for the damned; but here there is sometimes intermission of labor, and we receive comfort from our friends.

"Be careful at present, and sorrowful for your sins: that in the day of judgment, you may be secure with the blessed.

"*For then, the just shall stand with great constancy against those that afflicted and oppressed them* (Wis. 5:1).

"Then will he stand to judge, who now humbly submits himself to the judgment of men.

"Then, the poor and humble will have great confidence, and the proud will fear on every side."

"Learn at present to suffer little things, that then you may be delivered from more grievous sufferings.

"Try first here what you can not suffer hereafter.

"If you can now endure so little, how will you be able to bear everlasting torments?

"If a little suffering now makes you so impatient, what will hellfire do hereafter?

"Surely, you cannot have your pleasure in this world and afterwards reign with Christ.

✠ J.M.J. ✠

On Being Determined to
Amend Our Whole Life

(Thomas à Kempis, *Imitation of Christ,*
Book 1, Chapter 25)

"If to this day you had always lived in honors and pleasures, what would it avail you, if you were now in a moment to die?

"All then is vanity but to love God and to serve him alone!

"For he that loves God with his whole heart neither fears death, nor punishment, nor judgment, nor hell; because perfect love gives secure access to God.

"But he that is yet delighted with sin, no wonder if he be afraid of death and judgment." It is good, however, that if love as yet reclaim you not from evil, at least the fear of hell restrain you.

"But he that lays aside the fear of God will not be able to continue long in good, but will quickly fall into the snares of the devil."

"*Trust in the Lord, and do good, says the prophet, and inhabit the land, and thou shalt be fed with its riches* (Psalm 36:3).

"There is one thing which keep many back from spiritual progress and fervent amendment of life, and that is the apprehension of difficulty or the labor which must be gone through in the conflict.

"And they indeed advance most of all others in virtue, who strive manfully to overcome those things which they find more troublesome or contrary to them.

"For there, a man makes greater progress and merits greater grace, where he overcomes himself more and mortifies himself in spirit.

"But all men have not alike to overcome and mortify.

"Yet he that is diligent and zealous, although he have more passions to fight against, will be able to make a greater progress than another who has fewer passions, but is withal less fervent in the pursuit of virtue.

"Two things particularly conduce to a great amendment: these are, forcibly to withdraw one's self from that to which nature is viciously inclined, and earnestly to labor for that good which one wants the most."

✠ J.M.J. ✠

FIFTH MEDITATION

GIVING GLORY TO GOD IN THE WORLD

(St. John Henry Newman, *Parochial and Plain Sermons,* Vol. 8, Sermon 11)

"When persons are convinced that life is short, that it is unequal to any great purpose, that it does not display adequately, or bring to perfection the true Christian, when they feel that the next life is all in all and that eternity is the only subject that really can claim or can fill their thoughts, then they are apt to undervalue this life altogether and to forget its real importance. They are apt to wish to spend the time of their sojourning here in a positive separation from active and social duties: yet it should be recollected that the employments of this world, though not themselves heavenly, are, after all, the way to heaven – though not the fruit, are the seed of immortality – and are valuable, though not in themselves, yet for that to which they lead: but it is difficult to realize this. It is difficult to realize both truths at once, and to connect both truths together; steadily to contemplate the life to come, yet to act in this. Those who meditate are likely to neglect those active duties which are, in fact, incumbent on them, and to dwell upon the thought of God's glory, till they forget to act to His glory. This state of mind is chided in figure in the words of the Holy Angels to the Apostles, when they say, 'Men of Galilee, why do you stand looking up to heaven?' (Acts 1:11)

"In various ways does the thought of the next world lead men to neglect their duty in this; and whenever it does so, we may be sure that there is something wrong and unchristian, not in their thinking of the next world, but in their manner of thinking of it. For though the contemplation of God's glory may in certain times and persons allowably interfere with the active employments of life, as in the case of the Apostles when our Saviour ascended, and though such contemplation is even freely allowed or commanded us at certain times of each day, yet that is not a real and true meditation on Christ, but some counterfeit, which makes us dream away our time, or become habitually indolent, or which withdraws us from our existing duties, or unsettles us."

"I am speaking of case when it is a person's duty to remain in his worldly calling, and when he does remain in it, but when he cherishes dissatisfaction with it: whereas what he ought to feel is this – that while in it he is to glorify God, not out of it, but in it, and by means of it, according to the Apostle's direction, 'not slothful in zeal; be fervent in spirit, serving the Lord' (Rom.12:11). The Lord Jesus Christ, our Saviour, is best served, and with the most fervent spirit, when men are not slothful in business, but do their duty in that state of life in which it has pleased God to call them."

"... Bad as it is to be languid and indifferent in our secular duties and to account this religion, yet it is far worse to be the slaves of this world and to have our hearts in the concerns of this world ... I mean that ambitious spirit, to use a great word, but I know no other word to express my meaning – that low ambition which sets everyone on the lookout to succeed and to rise in life, to amass money, to gain power, to depress his rivals, to triumph over his hitherto superiors, to affect a consequence and a gentility which he had not before, to affect to have an opinion on high subjects, to pretend to form a judgment upon sacred things, to choose his religion, to approve and condemn according to his taste, to become a partisan in extensive measures for the supposed temporal benefit of the community, to indulge the vision of great things which are to come, great improvements, great wonders: all things vast, all things new-this most fearfully earthly and groveling spirit is likely, alas! to extend itself more and more among our countrymen – an intense, sleepless, restless, never-wearied, never-satisfied pursuit of Mammon in one shape or other, to the exclusion of all deep, all holy, all calm, all reverent thoughts. *This* is the spirit in which, more or less (according to their different tempers), men do commonly engage in concerns of this world; and I repeat it, better, far better, were it to retire from the world altogether than thus to engage in it – better with Elijah to fly to the desert, than to serve Baal and Ashtoreth in Jerusalem."

"But surely it is possible to 'serve the Lord,' yet not to be slothful in business; not over devoted to it, but not to retire from it. We may do all things whatever we are about to God's glory; we may do *all things heartily*, as to the Lord, and not to man, being both active yet meditative; and now let me give some instances to show what I mean.

"'Do all for the glory of God,' says St. Paul, in the text; nay, whether you eat or drink' (1 Cor. 10:31); so that it appears nothing is too slight or trivial to glory Him in. We will suppose then, to take the case mentioned just now; we will suppose a man who has lately had more serious thoughts than he had before and determines to live more religiously. In consequence of the turn, his mind has taken, he feels a distaste for his worldly occupation, whether he is in trade, or in any mechanical employment which allows little exercise of mind. He now feels he would rather be in some other business, though in itself his present occupation is quite lawful and pleasing to God. The ill-instructed man will at once get impatient and quit it; or if he does not quit it, at least he will be negligent and indolent in it. But the true penitent will say to himself, 'No; if it be an irksome employment, so much the more does it suit me. I deserve no better. I do not deserve to be fed even with husks. I am bound to afflict my soul for past sins. If I were to go in sackcloth and ashes, if I were to live on bread and water, if I were to wash the feet of the poor day by day, it would not be too great an humiliation; and the only reason I do not, is that I have no call that way, it would look ostentatious. Gladly then will I hail an inconvenience which will try me without anyone's knowing it. Far from repining, I will, through God's grace, go cheerfully about what I do not like. I will deny myself. I know that with His help, what is in itself painful will thus be pleasant as done towards Him. I know well that there is no pain but may be borne comfortably, by the thought of Him, and by His grace, and the strong determination of the will; nay, none but may soothe and solace me. Even the natural taste and smell may be made to like what they naturally dislike; even bitter medicine, which is nauseous to the palate, may by a resolute will become tolerable. Nay, even sufferings and torture, such as martyrs have borne, have before now been rejoiced in and embraced heartily from love to Christ. I then, a sinner, will take this light inconvenience in a generous way, pleased at the opportunity of disciplining myself, and with self-abasement, as needing a severe penitence. If there be parts in my occupation which I especially dislike, if it requires a good deal of moving about, and I wish to be at home, or if it be sedentary, and I wish to be in motion, or if it requires rising early, and I like to rise late, or if it makes me solitary, and I like to be with friends, all this unpleasant part, as far as is consistent with my health, and so that it is not likely to be a snare to me, I will choose by preference. Again, I see my religious views are a hindrance to me. I see persons are suspicious of me. I see that I offend people by my scrupulousness. I see that to get on in life requires far more devotion to my worldly business than I can give consistently with my duty to God, or without it becoming a temptation to me. I know that I ought not, and (please God) I will not, sacrifice my religion to it. My religious seasons and hours shall be my own. I will not countenance any of the worldly dealings and practices, the over-reaching ways, the sordid actions in which others indulge. And if I am thrown back in life thereby, if I make less gains or lose friends, and so come to be despised, and find others rise in the world while I remain where I was, hard though this be to bear, it is an humiliation which becomes me in requital for my sins, and in obedience to God; and a very slight one it is, merely to be deprived of worldly successes, or rather it is a gain. And this may be the manner in which Almighty God will make an opening for me, if it is His blessed will, to leave my present occupation. But leave it without a call from God, I certainly must not. On the contrary, I will work in it, the more diligently as far as higher duties allow me.' "

"Thankfulness to Almighty God, nay, and the inward life of the Spirit itself will be additional principles causing the Christian to labor diligently in his calling. He will see God in all things. He will recollect our Saviour's life. Christ was brought up to a humble trade. When he labors in his own, he will think of his Lord and Master in His. He will recollect that Christ went down to Nazareth and was subject to His parents, that He walked long journeys, that He bore the sun's heat and the storm, and had not where to lay His head. Again, he knows that the Apostles had various employments of this world before their calling; St. Andrew and St. Peter fishers, St. Matthew a tax-gatherer, and St. Paul, even after his calling, still a tent-maker. Accordingly, in whatever comes upon him, he will endeavor to discern and gaze (as it were) on the countenance of his Saviour. He will feel that the true contemplation of that Saviour lies in his worldly business; that as Christ is seen in the poor, and in the persecuted, and in children, so is He seen in the employments which He puts upon His chosen, whatever they be; that in attending to his own calling he will be meeting Christ; that if he neglects it, he will not on that account enjoy His presence at all the more, but that while performing it, he will see Christ revealed to his soul amid the ordinary actions of the day, as by a sort of sacrament. Thus he will take his worldly business as a gift from Him, and will love it as such."

"Still further, he will use his worldly business as a means of keeping him from vain and unprofitable thoughts. One cause of the heart's devising evil is, that time is given it to do so. The man who has his daily duties, who lays out his time for them hour by hour, is saved a multitude of sins which have not time to get hold upon him. The brooding over insults received, or the longing after some good not granted, or regret at losses which have befallen us, or at the loss of friends by death, or the attacks of impure and shameful thoughts, these are kept off from him who takes care to be diligent and well employed.

93

Leisure is the occasion of all evil. Idleness is the first step in the downward path, which leads to hell. If we do not find employment to engage our minds with, Satan will be sure to find his own employment for them. Here we see the differences of motive with which a religious and a worldly-minded man may do the same thing. Suppose a person has had some sad affliction, say a bereavement: men of this world, having no pleasure in religion, not liking to dwell on a loss to them irreparable, in order to drown reflection, betake themselves to worldly pursuits to divert their thoughts and banish gloom. The Christian under the same circumstances does the same thing, but it is from a fear lest he should relax and enfeeble his mind by barren sorrow; from a dread of becoming discontented; from a belief that he is pleasing God better, and is likely to secure his peace more fully, by not losing time; from a feeling that, far from forgetting those whom he has lost by thus acting, he shall only enjoy the thought of them the more really and the more religiously.

"Lastly, we see what judgment to give in a question sometimes agitated, whether one should retire from our worldly business at the close of life, to give our thoughts more entirely to God. To wish to do so is so natural that I suppose there is no one who would not wish it. A great many persons are not allowed the privilege, a great many are allowed it through increasing infirmities or extreme old age; but everyone, I conceive, if allowed to choose, would think it a privilege to be allowed it, though a great many would find it difficult to determine when was the fit time. But let us consider what is the reason of this so natural a wish. I fear that it is often not a religious wish, often only partially religious. I fear a great number of persons who whim at retiring from the world's business, do so under the notion of their then enjoying themselves somewhat after the manner of the rich man in the Gospel, who said, 'Soul, thou hast many good things laid up for many years' (Luke 12:19). If this is the predominant aim of anyone, of course, I need not say that it is a fatal sin, for Christ himself has said so. Others there are who are actuated by a mixed feeling; they are aware that they do not give so much time to religion as they ought; they do not live by rule; nay, they are not satisfied with the correctness or uprightness of some of the practices or customs which their way of life requires of them, and they get tired of active business as life goes on, and wish to be at ease. So they look to their last years as a time of retirement, in which they may both enjoy themselves and prepare for heaven. And thus they satisfy both their conscience and their love of the world. At present religion is irksome to them; but then, as they hope, duty and pleasure will go together. Now, putting aside all other mistakes which such a frame of mind evidences, let it be observed, that if they are at present not serving God with all their hearts, but look forward to a time when they shall do so, then it is plain that when at length they do put aside worldly cares and turn to God, if ever they do, that time must necessarily be a time of deep humiliation, if it is to be acceptable to Him, not a comfortable retirement. Whoever heard of a pleasurable, easy, joyous repentance? It is a contradiction in terms. These men, if they do but reflect a moment, must confess that their present mode of life, supposing it be not so strict as it should be, is heaping up tears and groans for their last years, not enjoyment. The longer they live as they do at present, not only the more unlikely is it that they will repent at all; but even if they do, the more bitter, the more painful must their repentance be. The only way to escape suffering for sin hereafter is to suffer for it here. Sorrow here or misery hereafter; they cannot escape one or the other.

"Not for any worldly reason, then, not on presumptuous or unbelieving motive, does the Christian desire leisure and retirement for his last years. Nay, he will be content to do with these blessings, and the highest Christian of all is he whose heart is so stayed on God, that he does not wish or need it; whose heart is so set on things above, that things below as little excite, agitate, unsettle, distress, and seduce him, as they stop the course of nature, as they stop the sun and moon, or change summer and winter. Such were the Apostles, who, as the heavenly bodies, went out to 'all nations' full of business, and yet full too of sweet harmony, even to the ends of the earth. Their calling was heavenly, but their work was earthly; they were in labor and trouble till the last; yet consider how calmly St. Paul and St. Peter write in their last days. St. John, on the other hand, was allowed in a great measure, to retire from the cares of his pastoral charge, and such, I say, will be the natural wish of every religious man, whether his ministry be spiritual or secular; but, not in order to begin to fix his mind on God, but merely because, though he may contemplate God as truly and be as holy in heart in active business as in quiet, still it is more becoming and suitable to meet the stroke of death (if it be allowed us) silently, collectively, solemnly, than in a crowd and a tumult. And hence it is, among other reasons that we pray in the Litany to be delivered 'from *sudden* death.'

"On the whole, then, what I have said comes to this, that whereas Adam was sentenced to labor as a punishment, Christ has by his coming sanctified it as means of grace and a sacrifice of thanksgiving, a sacrifice cheerfully to be offered up to the Father in His name."

"May God give us grace in our several spheres and stations to do His will and adorn His doctrine; that whether we eat and drink, or fast and pray, labor with our hands or with our minds, journey about or remain at rest, we may glorify Him who has purchased us with His own blood!"

✠ J.M.J. ✠

Prayer for the Storms of Life

(From The Raccolta)

"Thou seest, oh Lord, how on all sides the winds are let loose upon us, and the sea is growing rough with the violent commotion of the waves. Do thou, we beseech Thee, who alone art able, command the winds and the waves. Restore to mankind that true peace which the world cannot give, the peace which comes of good order. Let men impelled by thy grace return to a right and orderly course of life, practicing again, as they ought, love towards God, justice, and charity in dealing with their neighbor, temperance and self-control in their own lives. May thy kingdom come, and may those who now vainly and laboriously seek for truth and salvation, far removed from Thee, understand that they must live as thy servants in subjection to Thee. Thy laws show forth thy justice and paternal gentleness, and to enable us to keep them, Thou dost freely supply by thy grace the ready means. The life of man on earth is a warfare, but 'Thou dost thyself behold the strife, Thou dost help man to conquer, raise him when he falls, and crown him when he is victorious.' "

A Prayer That God's Will May Be Done

(Thomas à Kempis, *Imitation of Christ,*
Book 3, Chapter 15)

"Grant me your grace, most merciful Jesus, that it may be with me, and continue with me to the end.

"Grant me always to will and desire that which is most acceptable to you, and which pleases you best.

"Let your will be mine, and let my will always follow yours, and agree perfectly with it.

"Let me always will or not will the same with you: and let me not be able to will or not will otherwise than as you willest or willest not.

"Grant that I may die to all things that are in the world; and for your sake, love to be despised, and not to be known in this world.

"Grant that I may rest in you above all things desired and that my heart may be at peace in you.

"You are the true peace of heart; you are its only rest: outside of you, all things are hard and uneasy.

"*In this peace, in the self-same* that is in thee, the one sovereign, eternal God, *I will sleep, and I will rest.* Amen (Psalm 4:9)."

We Are Not To Trust In Men, But In God Alone

"Praise the Lord, O my soul, in my life, I will praise the Lord: I will sing to my God as long as I shall be.

"Put not your trust in princes: in the children of men, in whom there is no salvation.

"His spirit shall go forth, and he shall return into his earth: in that day, all their thoughts shall perish.

"Blessed is he who hath the God of Jacob for his helper, whose hope is in the Lord his God: who made heaven and earth, the sea, and all things that are in them.

"Who keepeth truth for ever: who executeth judgment for them that suffer wrong: who giveth food to the hungry.

"The Lord looseth them that are fettered: the Lord enlighteneth the blind.

"The Lord lifteth up them that are cast down: the Lord loveth the just.

"The Lord keepeth the strangers, he will support the fatherless and the widow: and the ways of sinners he will destroy.

"The Lord shall reign forever: thy God, O Sion, unto generation and generation" (Psalm 145).

✠ J.M.J. ✠

SIXTH MEDITATION

THE EUCHARIST, THE NEED OF OUR HEART

From St. Peter Julian Eymard,
The Real Presence)

Why is Jesus Christ in the Eucharist? "We might make several answers to this question. But that which comprises them all is this: He is there because He loves us, and because He desires that we love Him. Love – that is the reason of the institution of the Eucharist.

"Without the Eucharist, the love of Jesus Christ would be for us a dead love, a past love, which we should soon forget, and which we should be almost pardonable in forgetting. Love has its laws, its demands. The Eucharist alone fully satisfies them. By it, Jesus Christ has every right to be loved, because He testifies in its infinite love for us.

"Now, natural love, such as God has put into our hearts, demands three things: The presence of the loved one, or social life; community of goods; and perfect union.

"Absence is the pain of friendship, its torment. Distance weakens and, if it is too prolonged, ends by putting the firmest friendship to death.

"If our Lord is away from us, removed from us, our love for Him will undergo the dissolving effect of absence. It is in the nature of man's love to require, in order to live, the presence of the object loved.

"Behold the poor Apostles while Our Lord was in the tomb. The disciples of Emmaus avowed that they had almost lost faith because they no longer had their good Master.

"Ah! If our Lord had left us with no other pledge of His Love than Bethlehem and Calvary – poor Saviour! How quickly we should have forgotten Him! What indifference! "Love wishes to see, to hear, to converse, to touch.

"Nothing takes the place of the beloved one, neither souvenir, nor gifts, nor portraits. All that is without life.

"Our Lord knew it well. Nothing could have taken the place of His Person. We need Our Lord Himself.

"But His Word? No, it no longer sounds. We no longer hear the touching accents that fell from the lips of the Saviour.

"His Gospel? It is a testament.

"But His Sacraments – do they not give life? Ah! it takes the Author of Life to sustain it in us!

"The Cross? No; apart from Jesus, it only saddens!

"But hope? Without Jesus, it is agony!

"... Could Jesus have wished to reduce us to so sad a state of living and struggling without Him?

"Oh, we should be too unhappy without Jesus present with us! Exiled, alone upon earth, obliged to deprive ourselves of terrestrial goods, of the consolations of life, while the worldling has all that he desires – life would be insupportable!

"But with the Eucharist! With Jesus in the midst of us . . . by day and by night, accessible to all, waiting for everyone in His ever-open house, admitting the lowly, calling them with marked predilection – ah! Life is less bitter. He is the good Father in the midst of His children. It is social life with Jesus.

"And what society! Society that makes us better that elevates us! And what facilities for social relations with heaven, with Jesus Christ, Himself, in Person!

"It is, indeed, the sweet companionship of simple, loving, familiar, and intimate friendship.

"Ah! It was necessary!

"Love desires community of goods, common possession. It wishes to share happiness and unhappiness. To give is its nature, its instinct, to give all with joy, with pleasure. "And so, Jesus Christ in the Most Blessed Sacrament gives with profusion, with prodigality, His merits, His graces, yes, even His glory! Oh, how eager He is to give! He never refuses.

"And He gives Himself to all, and always.

"He covers the world with consecrated Hosts. He wishes all His children to possess Him. There still remain twelve baskets of the five loaves multiplied in the desert. All must have some!

"Jesus Christ would wish to envelop the world in His sacramental veil, to fertilize all nations in the waters of life that are losing themselves in the ocean of eternity, but only after having slaked the thirst, and strengthened the last of the elect.

"Ah! it is well for us, for all of us, O Jesus Eucharistic!

"Love tends to union, the union of them that love, the fusion of two into one, of two hearts into one heart, of two spirits into one, of two souls into one.

"... Jesus submitted to this law of love, which He had Himself established. After having shared our state, our life, He gives Himself in Communion; He absorbs us into Himself.

"Divine union of souls, always more perfect, always more intimate in proportion to the vivacity of our desires! *In me manet, et ego in eo. – He in me, and I in Him.* We abide in Him; He dwells in us. We make but one with Him until heaven consummates in eternal and glorious union, the ineffable union commenced here below by grace, and perfected by the Eucharist!

"Love lives, then, with Jesus present in the Most Blessed Sacrament. It shares all the riches of Jesus. It is united with Jesus.

"The needs of our heart are satisfied. It can demand no more.

"We Believe in the Love of God for Us. – Word of deep signification!

"Faith in the truth of the divine words and promises is exacted of every Christian. That is

110

simply faith. But the faith of love is higher and more perfect. It is the crown of the first.

"Faith in truth would be sterile if it did not lead to faith in love.

"What is that love in which we ought to believe?

"It is the love of Jesus Christ, the love which He testifies to us in the Eucharist, the love which is Himself, living and infinite love. "Happy they who believe in the love of Jesus Christ in the Eucharist! They love, for to believe is to love.

"They who are satisfied with believing in the truth of the Eucharist love, not at all or love very little. But what proofs of His love has Our Lord given in the Eucharist?

"In the first place, Our Lord has given us His word to that effect. He tells us that He loves us, that He has instituted His Sacrament only for love of us. Then, it is true.

"We believe an honorable man on his word. Why should we put less faith in that of Our Lord?

"When a friend desires to prove to his friend that he loves him, he tells him so, and he presses his hand affectionately.

"When Our Lord wants to show His love for us, He does so in person, discarding the intervention of any third person, whether angelic or human. Love suffers no intermediate agents.

"He remains in the Holy Eucharist that He may repeat to us incessantly: 'I love you! You must see that I love you!'

"Our Lord was so afraid that we would eventually forget Him that He took up His abode in the midst of us, made His home among us, placed His service within our reach so that we might not be able to think of Him without calling to mind His love. Giving Himself thus, He hoped, perhaps, not to be forgotten by men.

"Whoever reflects seriously on the Eucharist, but, above all, whoever participates in It, must feel convinced that Our Lord loves him. He feels that he has in Him a Father. He feels that he is loved as a child. He feels that he has the right to go to Him as to a Father and to speak freely with him. When in church, at the foot of the tabernacle, he is at home with his Father. He feels it.

"Ah! I understand why the Faithful love to live near churches, under the shadow of the paternal home.

"Thus, Jesus in the Most Blessed Sacrament tells us that He loves us. He repeats it to us interiorly and makes us feel it. Let us believe in His love.

"Does Jesus love us personally, individually?" To this question, there is but one answer: Do we belong to the Christian family? In a family, do not the father and the mother love each child with equal love? And if they had some preference, would it not be for the most delicate or infirm?

"Our Lord has for us the sentiment, at least, of a good Father.

"Why do we refuse Him that character?

"But still more, see how Our Lord exercises toward each one of us His personal love. He comes every morning to see each of His children, in particular, to visit him, speak to him, and embrace him. Although He comes so often, His visit is always as gracious, as loving as if it were the very first. He has not grown old. He is never tired of loving us, and of giving Himself to each of us.

"Does He not give Himself whole and entire to each one? And if the communicants are more numerous than the Hosts, does He not divide Himself for them? Does He ever give less to anyone?

"Even if the church is filled with adorers, cannot each one of us pray to Jesus, converse with Him? And is he not heard, is he not answered as favorably, as if he were alone in the church?

"Such is the personal love of Jesus. Everyone receives Him entire and does no wrong to anyone. As the sun sheds its light on each and all, as the ocean belongs entirely to each and all the fishes, so does Jesus belong to all of us. He is greater than all. He is inexhaustible.

"Another undeniable proof of the love of Our Lord is the persistence of that love in the Most Blessed Sacrament.

"How touching is this thought to the soul that understands! Numberless Masses are daily celebrated all over the world. They succeed one another almost without interruption. And how many of these Masses, in which Jesus offers Himself for us, are unattended, how many without assistants? While, on this new Calvary, Jesus is crying for mercy, sinners are outraging God and His Christ.

"Why does Our Lord renew His sacrifices so often, since we do not profit by it?

"Why does He remain day and night on our altars, to which no one comes to receive the graces that He is offering with full hands?

"Because He is loving, He is hoping, He is expecting! If Jesus came on our altars only on certain days, He would fear that some sinner, impelled by a desire to return to Him, might come seeking Him and, not finding Him, would go away without waiting for Him. So He prefers to await the sinner, long years Himself rather than make him wait an instant, rather than discourage him, perhaps, when he wants to escape from the slavery of sin.

"Oh, how few have even a remote idea of the love of Jesus in the Most Blessed Sacrament! And, nevertheless, it is true! Oh, we have no faith in the love of Jesus! Would we treat a friend, would we treat any man, as we do Our Lord?"

The Devout Soul Should Long Wholeheartedly For Union With Christ In The Sacrament

(Thomas à Kempis, *Imitation of Christ,*
Book 4, Chapter 13)

"Who will give me, O Lord, to find you alone, that I may open my whole heart to you and enjoy you as my soul desires; no one beholding me, nor any creature interesting me, or at all affecting me, but You alone speaking to me, and I to you, as the *Beloved* is wont to speak to his *Beloved*, and a friend to entertain himself with his friend.

"This I pray for, this I desire, that I may be wholly united to you, and may withdraw my heart from all created things; and by the Holy Communion ... may more and more learn to relish heavenly and eternal things.

"Ah! Lord God, when shall I be wholly united to and absorbed in you, and altogether forgetful of myself? You in me and I in you; and so grant us both to continue in one.

"Verily, you are my *Beloved*, the choicest among thousands, in whom my soul is well pleased to dwell all the days of my life.

"Verily, you are my Peacemaker, in whom is sovereign peace and true rest; out of whom is labor, and sorrow, and endless misery.

"You are, in truth, a hidden God, and your counsel is not with the wicked; but your conversation is with the humble and the simple.

"Oh! how sweet is your spirit, O Lord, who, to show your sweetness towards your children, vouchsafe to feed them with the most delicious bread which comes down from heaven.

"Surely there is no other nation so great, that has their God so near to them, as you, our God, are present to your faithful; to whom, for their daily comfort and for the raising up of their hearts to heaven, you give yourself to be eaten and enjoyed.

"For what other nation is there so honored as the Christian people?

"Or what creature under heaven so beloved as a devout soul, into whom God comes, that he may feed them with His glorious Flesh? O unspeakable grace! O wonderful condescension!

"O, infinite love! Singularly bestowed upon man.

"But what return shall I make to the Lord for this grace, and for so extraordinary a charity?

"There is nothing that I can give him that will please him better than if I give up my heart entirely to God, and unite it closely to him.

"Then all that is within me shall rejoice exceedingly, when my soul shall be perfectly united to my God; then will he say to me: If you will be with me, I will be with you; and I will answer him: Vouchsafe, O Lord, to remain with me, and I will willingly be with you.

"This is my whole desire that my heart may be united to you."

✠ J.M.J. ✠

OUR BLESSED MOTHER

Certain modern forms of Christianity speak of the Babe but never a word about the Mother of the Babe. The Babe of Bethlehem did not fall from the heavens into a bed of straw but came into this world through the great portals of the flesh. Sons are inseparable from mothers, and mothers inseparable from sons. Just as you cannot go to a statue of a mother holding a babe and cut away the mother, leaving the babe suspended in mid-air, neither can you cleave away the Mother from the Babe of Bethlehem. He was not suspended in mid-air in history, but, like all other babes, came into the world by and through His Mother. While we adore the Child, should we not then venerate His Mother, and while we kneel to Jesus, should we not at least clasp the hand of Mary for giving us such a Saviour? There is a grave danger that, lest in celebrating a Christmas without the Mother, we may soon reach a point where we will celebrate Christmas without the Babe, and these days are upon us now. And what an absurdity that is; for, just as there can never be a Christmas without a Christ, so there can never be a Christ without a Mary. Pull aside the curtain of the past, and under the light of Revelation, discover the role and interpret the part that Mary plays in the great Drama of Redemption!

Almighty God never launches a great work without exceeding preparation. The two greatest works of God are the Creation of the first man, Adam, and the Incarnation of the Son of God, the new Adam, Jesus Christ. But neither of these was accomplished without characteristic Divine preparation.

God did not make the masterpiece of creation, which was man, on the very first day, but deferred it until He had labored for six days in ornamenting the universe. From no material thing, but only by the fiat of His will, Omnipotence moved and said to Nothingness,

"Be"; and lo and behold, spheres fell into their orbits, passing one another in beautiful harmony, without ever a hitch or a halt. Then came the living things: The herbs bearing fruit as unconscious tribute to their Maker; the trees, with their leafy arms, outstretched all day in prayer; and the flowers, opening the chalice of their perfumes to their Creator. With the labor that was never exhausting, God then made the sensitive creatures to roam about, either in the watery palaces of the depths or on wings to fly through trackless space, or else as unwinged to roam the field in search of their repast and natural happiness. But all of this beauty, which has inspired the song of poets and the tracings of artists, was not in the Divine Mind sufficiently beautiful for the creature whom God would make the lord and master of the universe. He would do one thing more: He would set apart as a choice garden a small portion of His creation, beautify it with four rivers flowing through lands rich with gold and onyx, permit to roam in it the beasts of the field as domestics of that garden, in order to make it a paradise of the most intense happiness and pleasure possible to earth. When finally that Eden was made beautiful, as only God knows how to make things beautiful, He launched further the masterpiece of His creation, which was the first man, and in that paradise of pleasure was celebrated the first nuptials of humanity – the union of flesh and flesh of the first man and woman, Adam and Eve.

Now, if God so prepared for His first great work, which was man, by making the Paradise of Creation, it was even more fitting that before sending His Son to redeem the world, He should prepare for Him a Paradise of the Incarnation. And for many long centuries, He prepared it by symbols and the prophecies. In the language of types, He prepared human minds for some understanding of what this new Paradise would be. The burning bush of Moses inundated with the glory of God and conserving in the midst of its flame the freshness of its verdure and the perfume of its flowers, was a symbol of a new Paradise conserving in the honor of its maturity the very perfume of virginity. The rod of Aaron, flourishing in the solitude of the temple while isolated from the world by silence and retreat, was a symbol of that Paradise which, in a place of retirement and isolation from the world, would engender the very flower of the human race. The Ark of alliance, where the tables of the law were conserved, was a symbol of the new Paradise in which the Law in the Person of Christ would take up His very residence.

God prepared for that Paradise, not only by symbols but also by prophecies. Even in that dread day when an angel with a flaming sword was stationed in the first garden in creation, a prophecy was made that the serpent would not eventually conquer, but that a woman would crush its head. Later on, Isaiah and Jeremiah hailed that holy Paradise as one which would encircle a man.

But prophets and symbols were a too distant preparation. God would labor still more on His Paradise. He would make a Paradise not overrun with weeds and thistles, but blooming with every flower of virtue; a Paradise at the portals of which sin had never knocked, against the gates of which infidelity would never dare to storm; a Paradise from which would flow not four rivers through lands rich with gold and onyx, but four oceans of grace to the four corners of the world; a Paradise destined to bring forth the Tree of Life, and, therefore, full of life and grace itself; a Paradise in which was to be tabernacled Purity

125

itself, and therefore one immaculately pure; a Paradise so beautiful and sublime that the Heavenly Father would not have to blush in sending His Son into it. That flesh-gift Paradise of the Incarnation in which there were to be celebrated the nuptials, not of man and woman, but of humanity and divinity, is Our Own Beloved Mary, Mother of Our Lord and Saviour, Jesus Christ.

Why should not that Paradise of the Incarnation be spotless and pure? Why should she not be immaculate and stainless? Just suppose that you could have preexisted your own mother, in much the same way that an artist preexists his painting. Furthermore, suppose that you had an infinite power to make your mother anything that you pleased, just as a great artist like Raphael has the power of realizing his artistic ideals. Suppose you had this double power, what kind of mother would you have made for yourself? Would you have made her of such a type that would make you blush because of her unwomanly and unmotherlike actions? Would you have in any way stained and soiled her with the selfishness that would make her unattractive not only to you but to your fellow man? Would you have made her exteriorly and interiorly of such a character as to make you ashamed of her? Or would you have made her, so far as human beauty goes, the most beautiful woman in the world; and so far as beauty of soul goes, one who would radiate every virtue, every manner of kindness and charity and loveliness; one who by the purity of her life and her mind and her heart would be an inspiration not only to you but even to your fellow-men, so that all would look up to her as the very incarnation of what is best in motherhood? Now, if you, who are an imperfect being and who have not the most delicate conception of all that is fine in life, would have wished for the loveliest of mothers, do you think that our Blessed Lord, who not only preexisted His own mother but who had an infinite power to make her just what He chose, would, in virtue of all of the infinite delicacy of His spirit, make her any less pure and loving and beautiful than you would have made your own mother? If you who hate selfishness, and you who hate ugliness, would have made her beautiful, do you not think that the Son of God, who hates sin, would have made His own mother sinless, and He who hates moral ugliness would have made her immaculately beautiful?

Note how Sacred Scripture first implicitly and then explicitly reveals how Mary is the Mother of Christians. St. Luke, in recounting the birth of our Lord, says that Mary brought forth her "first-born." Certain critics have argued that this meant our Blessed Mother had other children according to the flesh, although in fact the Scriptures clearly indicate she was a virgin. The statement "first-born" may indeed mean that Mary was to have other children, not by the flesh but by the Spirit. It suggests that she was to have a spiritual progeny, which would make up the Mystical Body of her Divine Son, just as Eve is called the "mother of all living" or the mother of men in the natural order. Sara gave only one son to the father of believers, Abraham, and yet she is called the mother of all Israel. There is a clear suggestion in the words "first-born" that she who begot corporally the Head of the Church was also to beget spiritually the members of the Church. Since the Head and the Body are inseparable, it is, therefore, true to say that as Mary bore Christ in her womb, she was virtually carrying the whole Mystical Body. The mother earth that bears the vine also bears the branches.

When finally the Word is made flesh, and she brings Him to the temple on the fortieth day for purification, Mary's role in the Redemption becomes even clearer. Joseph was with her on that day, but the aged Simeon spoke only to her and reminded her that she was pierced by the sword of sorrow. Simeon, full of the prophetic spirit, was looking forward to the day when this Babe, the new Adam, would atone for sin on the Cross, as the Man of Sorrows, and where she as the new Eve would cooperate in that Redemption as the Woman of Sorrows. Simeon was practically telling her that Eden would become Calvary, the tree would be the Cross, and she would be the Mother of the Redeemer. But if she is the Mother of the Redeemer, then was she not called to be the Mother of the Redeemed? And if Christ was her first-born, would not the Redeemed be her other-born, brothers of Christ and sons of the heavenly Father?

All this became clearer when our Lord began to preach. One day as He was breaking the bread of truth to the multitude, someone in the crowd announced that His Blessed Mother was seeking Him. "But he answered and said to him who told him, 'Who is my mother?' . . . And, stretching forth his hand towards his disciples, he said, 'Behold my mother and my brethren! For whoever does the will of my Father in heaven, he is my brother and sister and mother'" (Matt. 12:48-50). These words did not mean a denial of His Blessed Mother, whom He loved next to His own heavenly Father; rather did they mean that there are other ties than those of the flesh. The world was being prepared for the fuller and deeper significance of the words "first-born." That day came on the Friday called Good and on a hill called Calvary. Our Lord had already given His garments to His executioners. Later on, He was to give His Body to the grave, and His Spirit to His Father. But He has two precious gifts yet to be conferred: His beloved disciple John and His sorrowful Mother, Mary. To whom could He give such gifts except to each other? And so to John, as representative of beloved redeemed humanity, He says: "Behold thy Mother." Then looking to His Mother, He said – not "Mother," but "Woman," to remind her of her universal relation to the race of the Redeemer – "Woman, behold thy son." "Behold thy son" – she had one Son already; He was hanging on the tree of ignominy. Now she was to have another; a son of Zebedee. John, then, was her second-born! All becomes clear. Her

Son told her there was another Motherhood than that of the flesh; now she realizes how literally true it was She brought forth her first-born in Bethlehem, and His name is Jesus; she brings forth her second-born on Calvary. Mary was destined to have other children than Jesus, but they were to be born not of her flesh but of her heart. Mother of Christ was she at the Cross. Her first-born in Bethlehem was brought forth in joy, but the curse of Eve hung about her labors at the Cross, for she was now, like Eve, bringing forth her children in sorrow. At that moment Mary suffered the pangs of spiritual childbirth for the millions of souls who would ever be called to the adoptive sonship of the Father, the brotherhood of Christ, and the joy of calling her Mother. The cup of her sorrow at the Cross, like her Son's, was filled to the brim, and no one knows how much she suffered to become our spiritual Mother or the Mother of the Mystical Body of her Divine Son. We only know that the millions of martyrs throughout all Christian ages consider their pains as insignificant compared to hers and scruple not to address her as the Queen of Martyrs.

✠ J.M.J. ✠

If Our Saviour could have thought of any better means of leading us back to Him, He would have put us in other hands than hers.

There are many falsehoods told about the Catholic Church. One of them is that Catholics adore Mary. This is absolutely untrue. Mary is a creature, human, not divine. Catholics do not adore Mary. That would be idolatry. But they do reverence her.

And to those Christians who have forgotten Mary, may we ask if it is proper for them to forget her whom He remembered on the Cross? Will they bear no love for that woman through the portals of whose flesh, as the Gate of Heaven, He came to earth?

One of the reasons why so many Christians have lost a belief in the Divinity of Christ is because they lost all affection for her upon whose white body, as a Tower of Ivory, that Infant climbed "to kiss upon her lips a mystic rose."

There is not a Christian in all the world who reverences Mary, who does not acknowledge Jesus her Son to be in Truth the Son of the Living

God. The prudent Christ on the Cross knew the prudent way to preserve belief in His Divinity, for who better than a Mother knows her son?

The gift of Mary did something to man, for it gave him an ideal love.

There has hardly ever been a mother in the history of the world who did not at one time or another say to her son or daughter: "Never do anything of which your mother would be ashamed."

The nobler the love, the nobler the character; and what nobler love could be given to men than the woman whom the Saviour of the world chose as His own Mother?

Why is it that the world has confessed its inability to inculcate virtue in the young? Very simply because it has not correlated morality to any love nobler than self-love. Things keep their proportion and fulfill their proper role only when integrated into a larger whole.

Most lives are like doors without hinges, or sleeves without coats, or bows without violins;

that is, unrelated to wholes or purposes which give them meaning.

The modern emphasis on sex is a result of tearing a function away from a purpose, a part away from a whole. It can never be handled properly unless integrated to a larger pattern and made to serve it.

That is, to some extent, the role Our Blessed Mother plays in the moral life of our Catholic youth. She is that ideal love for which lesser and baser loves and impulses are sacrificed.

The level of any civilization is the level of its womanhood. What they are, men will be, for love always goes out to meet the demands of the object loved. Given a woman like the Mother of Our Lord as our supernatural Mother, we have one of the greatest inspirations for nobler living this world has ever known.

✠ J.M.J. ✠

Salve Regina

Hail Holy Queen, Mother of Mercy. Hail our life, our sweetness, and our hope! To thee do we cry, poor banished children of Eve; to thee do we send up our sighs, mourning, and weeping in this vale of tears. Turn, then, most gracious advocate, thine eyes of mercy toward us; and after this our exile, show unto us the blessed fruit of thy womb, Jesus. O clement, O loving, O sweet Virgin Mary. Pray for us, O holy Mother of God. That we may be made worthy of the promises of Christ. Amen.

Hail Mary

Hail Mary, full of grace, the Lord is with thee: blessed art thou amongst women, and blessed is the fruit of thy womb, Jesus. Holy Mary, Mother of God, pray for us sinners, now and at the hour of our death. Amen.

✠ J.M.J. ✠

Litany of the Blessed Virgin Mary

Lord, have mercy on us.

Christ, have mercy on us.

Lord, have mercy on us.

Christ, hear us.

Christ, graciously hear us.

God the Father of heaven, have mercy on us.

God the Son, Redeemer of the world, have mercy on us.

God, the Holy Spirit, have mercy on us.

Holy Trinity, one God, have mercy on us.

Holy Mary, pray for us.

Holy Mother of God, pray for us.

Holy Virgin of virgins, pray for us.

Mother of Christ, pray for us.

Mother of divine grace, pray for us.

Mother most pure, pray for us.

Mother most chaste, pray for us.

Mother inviolate, pray for us.

Mother undefiled, pray for us.

Mother most amiable, pray for us.

Mother most admirable, pray for us.

Mother of good counsel, pray for us.

Mother of our Creator, pray for us.

Mother of our Saviour, pray for us.

Virgin most prudent, pray for us.

Virgin most venerable, pray for us.

Virgin most renowned, pray for us.

Virgin most powerful, pray for us.

Virgin most merciful, pray for us.

Virgin most faithful, pray for us.

Mirror of justice, pray for us.

Seat of wisdom, pray for us.

Cause of our joy, pray for us.

Spiritual vessel, pray for us.

Vessel of honor, pray for us.

Singular vessel of devotion, pray for us.

Mystical Rose, pray for us.

Tower of David, pray for us.

Tower of ivory, pray for us.

House of gold, pray for us.

Ark of the covenant, pray for us.

Gate of heaven, pray for us.

Morning star, pray for us.

Health of the sick, pray for us.

Refuge of sinners, pray for us.

Comforter of the afflicted, pray for us.

Help of Christians, pray for us.

Queen of angels, pray for us.

Queen of patriarchs, pray for us.

Queen of prophets, pray for us.

Queen of apostles, pray for us.

Queen of martyrs, pray for us.

Queen of confessors, pray for us.

Queen of virgins, pray for us.

Queen of all saints, pray for us.

Queen conceived without original sin, pray for us.

Queen of the most holy Rosary, pray for us.

Queen of peace, pray for us.

Lamb of God, who takes away the sins of the world.
Spare us, O Lord.

Lamb of God, who takes away the sins of the world.

Graciously hear us, O Lord.

Lamb of God, who takes away the sins of the world.

Have mercy on us.

Christ, hear us.

Christ, graciously hear us.

Pray for us, O holy Mother of God.

That we may be made worthy of the promises of Christ.

Let Us Pray

Pour forth, we beseech thee, O Lord, Thy grace into our hearts; that we to whom the incarnation of Christ Thy Son was made known by the message of an angel, may by His passion and cross be brought to the glory of His resurrection. Through the same Christ our Lord.

May the divine assistance remain always with us.

May the souls of the faithful departed, through the mercy of God, rest in peace. Amen.

We fly to thy patronage, O holy Mother of God, despise not our petitions in our necessities; but deliver us from all dangers, O ever glorious and blessed Virgin. Amen.

"To Our Lady"
(Lovely Lady Dressed in Blue)

Lovely Lady dressed in blue
Teach me how to pray!
God was just your little Boy,
Tell me what to say!

Did you lift Him up, sometimes,
Gently, on your knee?
Did you sing to Him the way
Mother does to me?

Did you hold His hand at night?
Did you ever try
Telling stories of the world?
O! And did He cry?

Do you really think He cares
If I tell Him things —
Little things that happen? And
Do the Angels' wings

Make a noise? And can He hear
Me if I speak low?
Does He understand me now?
Tell me — for you know?

Lovely Lady dressed in blue
Teach me how to pray!
God was just your little Boy,
And you know the way.

(Mary Dixon Thayer)

PRAYERS OF

MEDITATION AND PETITION

FROM THE ARMOR OF GOD

&

HOLY HOUR BOOKLETS

Christic to a Faithful Soul

9-16-24

(Thomas à Kempis, *The Imitation of Christ*,
Book 3, Chapter 1)

Happy are the souls that hear the Lord speaking within them, and from their mouths receive the word of comfort.

Happy are the ears that hear the accents of the divine whisper and take no notice of the whisperings of the world.

Happy ears, indeed, are those ears that hearken to truth itself teaching within, and who hearken not to the voice that sounds without.

Happy eyes that are shut to outward things and attentive to the interior. Happy they who penetrate into internal things and endeavor to prepare themselves more and more by daily exercises, the attaining to heavenly secrets.

Happy are they who seek to be wholly intent on God and who rid themselves of every worldly impediment.

Mind these things, O my soul, and shut the doors of your senses, that you may hear what the Lord your God speaks within you.

Thus says your Beloved: I am your salvation, your peace, and your life; abide in me, and you shall find peace.

Leave alone all transitory things, and seek things eternal.

What are all temporal things, but deceit? And what will all things created avail you, if you be forsaken by your Creator?

Cast off, then, all earthly things; make yourself agreeable to your Creator and faithful to Him so that you may attain to true happiness.

✠ J.M.J. ✠

Prayer to Follow the Example
of Jesus Christ

(Thomas à Kempis, *The Imitation of Christ,*
Book 3, Chapter 18)

My Child, I came down from heaven for
your salvation; I took upon me your miseries, not
of necessity, but moved out of love, that you
might learn patience, and might bear, without
repining, the miseries of this life. For, from the
hour of my birth till my expiring on the Cross, I
was never without suffering.

Lord, because You were patient in life,
especially in fulfilling the commandment of the
Father, it is fitting that I, a wretched sinner,
should, according to Your will, take all with
patience and, as long as You wish, support the
burden of this corruptible life, in order to gain my
salvation.

Oh, what great thanks am I obliged to
return to You for having vouchsafed to show me

and all the faithful a right and good way to an everlasting kingdom.

Had You not gone before and instructed us, who would have cared to follow?

Behold, we are still tepid, notwithstanding all the miracles and instructions we have heard. What, then, would it be, if we had not this great light whereby to follow You?

Prayer Against Evil Thoughts

(Thomas à Kempis, *The Imitation of Christ*,
Book 3, Chapter 23)

O Lord, my God, be not far from me. O my God, hasten to help me, for diverse evil thoughts and great fears have risen up against me, afflicting my soul. How shall I pass them without hurt? How shall I break through them?

"And the people shall take them, and bring them into their place: and the house of Israel shall possess them in the land of the Lord for servants and handmaids: and they shall make them captives that had taken them, and shall subdue their oppressors" (Isa. 14:2).

I, saith He, will go before thee, and will humble the great ones of the earth. I will open the gates of the prison and reveal to thee hidden secrets.

Do, as you say, Lord, and let all these wicked thoughts flee from Your face.

This is my hope and my only comfort, to fly to You in all tribulations, to confide in You, to call on You from my heart, and patiently to look for Your consolation.

✠ J.M.J. ✠

Prayer for the Enlightening of the Mind

(Thomas à Kempis, *The Imitation of Christ,*
Book 3, Chapter 23)

Enlighten me, O good Jesus, with the brightness of internal light, and cast all darkness from the dwelling of my heart. Restrain my many wandering thoughts, and suppress all of the temptations that violently assault me.

Fight strongly for me, and overcome these wicked beasts — I mean these alluring concupiscences — that peace may be made in Your power, and the abundance of Your praise may resound in Your holy court, which is a clean conscience.

Command the winds and storms; say to the sea, "Be still" and to the north wind, "Blow thou not"; and a great calm shall ensue.

Send forth Your light and Your truth to shine upon the earth; for I am as the earth, empty and void until You illumine me.

Pour out Your grace from above; water my heart with the dew of heaven. Send down the waters of devotion to wash the face of the earth, to bring forth good and perfect fruit.

Lift up my mind, oppressed with the load of sins, and raise my whole desire toward heavenly things, that, having tasted the sweetness of the happiness above, I may have no pleasure in thinking of the things of the earth.

Draw me away, and deliver me from all unstable comfort of creatures; for no created thing can fully quiet and satisfy my desires.

Join me to Yourself by an inseparable bond of love, because You alone can satisfy the lover, and without You, all things are frivolous.

✠ J.M.J. ✠

Prayer for Charity and Tolerance

(Attributed to Eusebius, Bishop of Caesarea)

May I be no man's enemy, and may I be the friend of that which is eternal and abides. May I never quarrel with those nearest me; and if I do, may I be reconciled quickly. May I never devise evil against any man; if any devise evil against me, may I escape uninjured and without the need of hurting him.

May I love, seek, and attain only that which is good. May I wish for all men's happiness and envy none. May I never rejoice in the ill-fortune of one who has wronged me.

When I have done or said what is wrong, may I never wait for the rebuke of others, but always rebuke myself until I make amends. May I win no victory that harms either me or my opponent. May I reconcile friends who are angry with one another.

May I, to the extent of my power, give all needful help to my friends and to all who are in want. May I never fail a friend in danger.

When visiting those in grief, may I be able, by gentle and healing words, to soften their pain.

May I respect myself . . . May I always tame that which rages within me . . .

May I accustom myself to be gentle and never be angry with people because of circumstances.

May I never discuss who is wicked and what wicked things he has done, but know good men and follow in their footsteps, through Christ Our Lord. Amen.

✠ J.M.J. ✠

A Universal Prayer

(Composed by Pope Clement XI)

O my God, I believe in Thee; do Thou strengthen my faith. All my hopes are in Thee; do Thou secure them. I love Thee with my whole heart; teach me to love Thee daily more and more. I am sorry that I have offended Thee; do Thou increase my sorrow.

I adore Thee as my first beginning; I aspire after Thee as my last end. I give Thee thanks as my constant benefactor; I call upon Thee as my sovereign protector.

Vouchsafe, O my God, to conduct me by Thy wisdom, to restrain me by Thy justice, to comfort me by Thy mercy, to defend me by Thy power.

To Thee I desire to consecrate all my thoughts, words, actions, and sufferings; that henceforward I may think of Thee, speak of Thee, constantly refer all my actions to Thy greater glory, and suffer willingly whatever Thou shall appoint.

Lord, I desire in all things that Thy will may be done, because it is Thy will, in the manner Thou willest, and for as long as willest.

I beg of Thee to enlighten my understanding, to inflame my will, to purify my body, and to sanctify my soul.

Grant that I be not puffed up with pride, moved by flattery, deceived by the world, or duped by the devil.

Give me grace to purify my memory, to bridle my tongue, to restrain my eyes, and to mortify my senses.

Give me strength, O my God, to expiate my offenses, to overcome my temptations, to subdue my passions, and to acquire the virtues proper for my state.

Fill my heart with a tender affection for Thy goodness, a hatred for my faults, a love for my neighbor, and a contempt for the world.

Let me always remember to be submissive to my superiors, patient with my inferiors, faithful to my friends, and charitable to my enemies.

Grant, O Jesus, that I may remember Thy precept and example by loving my enemies, bearing with injuries, doing good to those who persecute me, and praying for those who slander me.

Assist me to overcome sensuality by mortification, avarice by almsdeeds, anger by meekness, and tepidity by devotion.

O my God, make me prudent in my undertakings, courageous in dangers, patient in afflictions, and humble in prosperity.

Grant that I may be ever attentive in my prayers, temperate at meals, diligent in employments, and constant in good resolutions.

Let my conscience be ever upright and pure, my exterior modest, my conversation edifying, and my life according to rule.

Assist me, that I may continually labor to overcome nature, to correspond with Thy grace, to keep Thy commandments, and to work out my salvation.

Help me to obtain holiness of life by a sincere confession of my sins, by a devout reception of the Body of Christ, by a continual recollection of mind, and by a pure intention of heart.

Reveal to me, O my God, the nothingness of this world, the greatness of heaven, the shortness of time, and the length of eternity.

Grant that I may prepare for death, that I may fear Thy judgments, that I may escape hell and, in the end, obtain heaven, through the merits of Our Lord Jesus Christ.

✠ J.M.J. ✠

A Prayer of the Church Under Grievous Persecutions

Thou hast broken up the fountains and the torrents; thou hast dried up the Ethan rivers.

Thine is the day, and thine is the night; thou hast made the morning light and the sun.

Thou hast made all the borders of the earth; the summer and the spring were formed by thee.

Remember this, the enemy hath reproached the Lord; and a foolish people hath provoked thy name.

Deliver not up to beasts the souls that confess to thee, and forget not to the end the souls of thy poor.

Have regard to thy covenant, for they that are the obscure of the earth have been filled with dwellings of iniquity.

Let not the humble be turned away with confusion; the poor and needy shall praise thy name.

Arise, O God, judge thy own cause: remember thy reproaches with which the foolish man hath reproached thee all the day.

Forget not the voices of thy enemies — the pride of them that hate thee ascendeth continually. (Ps. 73 [74]:15–23)

Prayer of St. Ignatius

Take, O Lord, and receive my entire liberty, my memory, my understanding, and my whole will. All that I am, all that I have, Thou hast given me, and I will give it back again to Thee to be disposed of according to Thy good pleasure. Give me only Thy love and Thy grace; with Thee, I am rich enough, nor do I ask for aught besides. Amen.

ACKNOWLEDGMENTS

To the members of the Archbishop Fulton John Sheen Foundation in Peoria, Illinois. In particular, to the Most Rev. Daniel R. Jenky, C.S.C., Bishop of Peoria, for your leadership and fidelity to the cause of Sheen's canonization and the creation of this book.

www.archbishopsheencause.org

To Phillip Lee from the Catholic Diocese of Peoria for granting permission to use the picture of the Sacred Host in the monstrance, which was placed on the main altar at the Cathedral of St. Mary of the Immaculate Conception located in Peoria, Illinois.

(www.cdop.org)

To the staff at Sophia Institute Press for their invaluable assistance in sharing the writings of Archbishop Fulton J. Sheen to a new generation of readers.

www.sophiainstitute.com

To the volunteers at the Archbishop Fulton J. Sheen Mission Society of Canada: your motto "Unless Souls are Saved, Nothing is Saved", speaks to the reality that Jesus Christ came into the world to make salvation available to all souls.

www.archbishopfultonjsheenmissionsocietyofcanada.org

To the good folks at 'Bishop Sheen Today'. We value your guidance, support, and prayers in helping us to share the wisdom of Archbishop Fulton J. Sheen. Your apostolic work of sharing his audio and video presentations along with his many writings to a worldwide audience is very much appreciated.

www.bishopsheentoday.com

And lastly, to Archbishop Fulton J. Sheen, whose teachings on Our Lord's Passion and His Seven Last Words continue to inspire me to love God more and to appreciate the gift of the Church. May we be so blessed as to imitate Archbishop Sheen's love for the saints, the sacraments, the Eucharist, and the Blessed Virgin Mary. May the Good Lord grant him a very high place in heaven!

✠ J.M.J. ✠

ABOUT THE AUTHOR
Fulton J. Sheen
(1895–1979)

ARCHBISHOP SHEEN, best known for his popularly televised and syndicated television program, Life is Worth Living, is held today as one of Catholicism's most widely recognized figures of the twentieth century.

Fulton John Sheen, born May 8, 1895, in El Paso, Illinois was raised and educated in the Roman Catholic faith. Originally named Peter John Sheen, he came to be known as a young boy by his mother's maiden name, Fulton. He was ordained a priest of the Diocese of Peoria at St. Mary's Cathedral in Peoria, IL on September 20, 1919.

Following his ordination, Sheen studied at the Catholic University of Louvain, where he earned a doctorate in philosophy in 1923. That same year, he received the Cardinal Mercier Prize for International Philosophy, becoming the first-ever American to earn this distinction.

Upon returning to America, after varied and extensive work throughout Europe, Sheen continued to preach and teach theology and philosophy from 1927 to 1950, at the Catholic University of America in Washington DC.

Beginning in 1930, Sheen hosted a weekly Sunday night radio broadcast called 'The Catholic Hour'. This broadcast captured many devoted listeners, reportedly drawing an audience of four million people every week for over twenty years.

In 1950, he became the National Director of the Society for the Propagation of the Faith, raising funds to support missionaries. During the sixteen years that he held this position, millions of dollars were raised to support the missionary activity of the Church. These efforts influenced tens of millions of people all over the world, bringing them to know Christ and his Church. In addition, his preaching and personal example brought about many converts to Catholicism.

In 1951, Sheen was appointed Auxiliary Bishop of the Archdiocese of New York. That same year, he began hosting his television program 'Life is Worth Living', which lasted for six years.

In the course of its run, that program competed for airtime with popular television programs hosted by the likes of Frank Sinatra and Milton Berle. Sheen's program held its own, and in 1953, just two years after its debut, he won an Emmy Award for "Most Outstanding Television Personality." Fulton Sheen credited the Gospel writers - Matthew, Mark, Luke, and John - for their valuable contribution to his success. Sheen's television show ran until 1957, boasting as many as thirty million weekly viewers.

In the Fall of 1966, Sheen was appointed Bishop of Rochester, New York. During that time, Bishop Sheen hosted another television series, 'The Fulton Sheen Program' which ran from 1961 to 1968, closely modeling the format of his 'Life is Worth Living' series.

After nearly three years as Bishop of Rochester, Fulton Sheen resigned and was soon appointed by Pope Paul VI as Titular Archbishop of the See of Newport, Wales. This new appointment allowed Sheen the flexibility to continue preaching.

Another claim to fame was Bishop Sheen's annual Good Friday homilies, which he preached for fifty-eight consecutive years at St. Patrick's Cathedral in New York City, and elsewhere. Sheen also led numerous retreats for priests and religious, preaching at conferences all over the world.

When asked by Pope St. Pius XII how many converts he had made, Sheen responded, "Your Holiness, I have never counted them. I am always afraid that if I did count them, I might think I made them, instead of the Lord."

Sheen was known for being approachable and down to earth. He used to say, "If you want people to stay as they are, tell them what they want to hear. If you want to improve them, tell them what they should know." This he did, not only in his preaching but also through his numerous books and articles. His book titled 'Peace of Soul' was sixth on the New York Times best-seller list.

Three of Sheen's great loves were: the missions and the propagation of the faith; the Holy Mother of God and the Eucharist.

He made a daily holy hour of prayer before the Blessed Sacrament. It was from Jesus Himself that he drew strength and inspiration to preach the gospel, and in the Presence of Whom that he prepared his homilies. "I beg [Christ] every day to keep me strong physically and alert mentally, in order to preach His gospel and proclaim His Cross and Resurrection," he said. "I am so happy doing this that I sometimes feel that when I come to the good Lord in Heaven, I will take a few days' rest and then ask Him to allow me to come back again to this earth to do some more work."

His contributions to the Catholic Church are numerous and varied, ranging from educating in classrooms, churches, and homes, to preaching over a nationally publicized radio show, and two television programs, as well as penning over sixty written works. Archbishop Fulton J. Sheen had a gift for communicating the Word of God in the most pure, simple way. His strong background in philosophy helped him to relate to everyone in a highly personalized manner. His timeless messages continue to have great relevance today. His goal was to inspire everyone to live a God-centered life with the joy and love that God intended.

On October 2, 1979, Archbishop Sheen received his greatest accolade, when Pope St. John Paul II embraced him at St. Patrick's Cathedral in New York City. The Holy Father said to him, "You have written and spoken well of the Lord Jesus. You are a loyal son of the Church."

The good Lord called Fulton Sheen home on December 9, 1979. His television broadcasts now available through various media, and his books, extend his earthly work of winning souls for Christ. Sheen's cause for canonization was opened in 2002. In 2012, Pope Benedict XVI declared him 'Venerable', and in July of 2019, Pope Francis formally approved the miracle necessary for Sheen's beatification and canonization process to move forward. The time and date for the church to declare Archbishop Fulton J. Sheen a saint is in God's hands.

Quality Books Available Through
Bishop Sheen Today Publishing

For God and Country

Calvary and the Mass

The Cross and the Beatitudes

The Cross and the Crisis

Liberty, Equality and Fraternity

The Rainbow of Sorrow

Victory Over Vice

The Seven Virtues

Seven Pillars of Peace

God and War

The Divine Verdict

Missions and the World Crisis

God Love You

The Seven Last Words Explained

The Priest Is Not His Own

The Cross and the Crib

Philosophies at War

Seven Words to the Cross

Love One Another

Seven Words of Jesus & Mary

www.bishopsheentoday.com

✠ J.M.J. ✠